D1716295

ASVAB
TEST PREP

The Most Complete and Powerful Study Guide
to Prepare for the Current Exam in Just
1 Week and Score 99 on the AFQT
at Your First Try

Ryan MacArmen

- SPEED PREP ACADEMY -

© Copyright - All rights reserved.

The content contained within this book may not be reproduced, duplicated or transmitted without direct written permission from the author or the publisher.

Under no circumstances will any blame or legal responsibility be held against the publisher, or author, for any damages, reparation, or monetary loss due to the information contained within this book. Either directly or indirectly.

Legal Notice:

This book is copyright protected. This book is only for personal use. You cannot amend, distribute, sell, use, quote or paraphrase any part, or the content within this book, without the consent of the author or publisher.

Disclaimer Notice:

Please note the information contained within this document is for educational and entertainment purposes only. All effort has been executed to present accurate, up to date, and reliable, complete information. No warranties of any kind are declared or implied. Readers acknowledge that the author is not engaging in the rendering of legal, financial, medical or professional advice. The content within this book has been derived from various sources. Please consult a licensed professional before attempting any techniques outlined in this book.

By reading this document, the reader agrees that under no circumstances is the author responsible for any losses, direct or indirect, which are incurred as a result of the use of information contained within this document, including, but not limited to, — errors, omissions, or inaccuracies.

ACCESS YOUR GIFTS!

ASVAB Exam Video Lessons
ASVAB Exam Simulator
ASVAB Exam Flashcards

SCAN THIS QR CODE TO ACCESS 'EM

For any scanning or accessing problem do not hesitate to contact my support at this email:
info@speedprepacademy.com

Contents

Preface

Welcome to this comprehensive guide designed to prepare you for the Armed Services Vocational Aptitude Battery (ASVAB). As you stand at the threshold of a potential career in the United States Armed Forces, this guide aims to be your steadfast companion, offering clarity, direction, and in-depth knowledge for the journey ahead.

Why This Guide Matters

The decision to join the military is a significant one, marked by a commitment to service, discipline, and growth. The ASVAB is a crucial step in this journey, serving as a gateway to understanding your strengths and aligning them with the needs and opportunities within the military. This guide is crafted not only to help you excel in the ASVAB but also to provide a deeper understanding of the skills and knowledge essential for a successful military career.

What to Expect

Within these pages, you'll find:

Detailed Overviews: Each section of the ASVAB is broken down into digestible parts, explaining key concepts and subject areas.
Practical Strategies: From tackling specific types of questions to managing time and stress, this guide offers practical strategies tailored to each part of the test.
Real-World Applications: We go beyond mere test preparation, highlighting the real-world applications of the skills and knowledge you're developing.
Personal Insights: Drawing on my experience and that of others in the military, the guide offers personal insights and tips that resonate with your aspirations.

Your Role in This Journey

As you engage with this guide, remember that your attitude, dedication, and effort are pivotal. The journey to excelling on the ASVAB is as much about hard work and determination as it is about intelligence and ability. Use this guide not just as a resource, but as a tool to actively engage with and challenge your understanding.

Beyond the Test

While the primary focus is to prepare you for the ASVAB, the ultimate goal is to equip you with knowledge and skills that will benefit you in military training and throughout your career. The disciplines you embrace and the knowledge you acquire here will serve as a foundation upon which much of your military career will be built.

Final Thoughts

As you turn each page, approach the content with an open mind and a commitment to absorb and apply the knowledge. This guide is more than a preparation for a test; it's a preparation for a significant and rewarding path in life.

Thank you for choosing this guide as your companion on this journey. May it lead you to success on the ASVAB and in the many challenges and triumphs that await in your future service to our nation.

Let the journey begin!

Ryan MacArmen

INTRODUCTION

Welcome to the beginning of a pivotal journey in your career and life. This guide is designed to introduce you to the Armed Services Vocational Aptitude Battery (ASVAB) Test, a key milestone for anyone aspiring to join the United States Armed Forces. The ASVAB is more than just an exam; it is a comprehensive assessment that evaluates your strengths, aptitudes, and potential for success in military training and careers.

ASVAB Test Overview

Understanding the structure and format of the Armed Services Vocational Aptitude Battery (ASVAB) is crucial for any prospective service member. The ASVAB is administered in two primary formats: the Computerized Adaptive Testing (CAT) ASVAB and the Paper & Pencil (P&P) ASVAB. Both versions aim to assess a candidate's qualifications for enlistment in the United States armed forces and determine suitability for various military occupations.

CAT-ASVAB

The CAT-ASVAB is an adaptive test administered at Military Entrance Processing Stations (MEPS) and some Military Entrance Test (MET) sites. The key features of this format are:

- **Adaptive Testing:** The difficulty of the test adjusts based on the test-taker's responses. Correct answers lead to harder questions, while incorrect answers lead to easier ones. This method helps in accurately gauging the individual's ability level.
- **Time-Efficient:** Since the test adapts to one's ability level, it generally takes less time than the P&P version.
- **Immediate Scoring:** Results are calculated instantly upon test completion, offering immediate feedback on performance.
- **Sections and Questions:** The CAT-ASVAB includes nine subtests: General Science, Arithmetic Reasoning, Word Knowledge, Paragraph Comprehension, Mathematics Knowledge, Electronics Information, Auto Information, Shop Information, and Mechanical Comprehension.

P&P-ASVAB

The Paper & Pencil ASVAB is offered at schools and MEPS for individuals who do not have access to the computerized version. Its characteristics include:

- **Fixed Questions:** Unlike the CAT-ASVAB, the difficulty level does not adapt to the test-taker's responses. Each candidate receives a fixed set of questions.
- **Standardized Testing Environment:** It offers a more traditional testing environment, which some test-takers may prefer or find less stressful.
- **Manual Scoring:** The tests are sent to be scored, so results are not immediately available.
- **Sections and Questions:** It covers the same nine subtests as the CAT-ASVAB but with a fixed number of questions and time limits for each section.

Preparing for Both Formats

Regardless of the format, preparation for the ASVAB requires a solid understanding of the content areas covered by the test. Prospective test-takers should focus on:

- **Studying Subject Areas:** Review the subjects in each subtest thoroughly.
- **Practice Tests:** Take practice tests to familiarize oneself with the format and type of questions asked.
- **Time Management:** Learn to manage time effectively, especially for the P&P ASVAB.
- **Stress Management:** Develop techniques to stay calm and focused, which is particularly useful for the adaptive nature of the CAT-ASVAB

Purpose of the ASVAB

The ASVAB serves a dual purpose:

- **Eligibility for Enlistment:** It determines your qualification for enlistment in the U.S. military.
- **Career Exploration:** The test helps identify which military occupations or specialties align with your skills and interests.

Structure of the ASVAB

The ASVAB is composed of multiple subtests, each designed to measure different skill sets:

- **General Science:** Knowledge of physical and biological sciences.
- **Arithmetic Reasoning:** Aptitude in basic arithmetic and problem-solving.
- **Word Knowledge:** Understanding and recognition of vocabulary.
- **Paragraph Comprehension:** Ability to interpret written information.
- **Mathematics Knowledge:** Proficiency in mathematical concepts and applications.
- **Electronics Information:** Understanding of electrical systems and electronics.
- **Auto and Shop Information:** Knowledge of automotive maintenance and repair, as well as wood and metal shop work.
- **Mechanical Comprehension:** Comprehension of mechanical principles and physical laws.
- **Assembling Objects:** Spatial visualization and ability to discern how parts fit together.

Formats of the ASVAB

The ASVAB is available in two formats:

- **Computerized Adaptive Test (CAT-ASVAB):** Taken at Military Entrance Processing Stations (MEPS) and Military Entrance Test (MET) sites, this version adapts the difficulty of questions on your responses.
- **Paper & Pencil (P&P ASVAB):** Offered at various locations, including high schools and colleges.

Preparing for the ASVAB

Preparation for the ASVAB is crucial for achieving the best possible scores. This guide is crafted to assist you in that preparation, offering detailed insights into each subtest, strategies for tackling different types of questions, and methods to manage time and stress effectively.

The Journey Ahead

Embarking on the ASVAB is the first step toward a fulfilling and honorable career in the military. It is an opportunity to discover and showcase your abilities, and to pave the path for your future role in serving and protecting the nation.

In this guide, we will walk you through each aspect of the ASVAB, equipping you with the knowledge and confidence to approach the test with a prepared and positive mindset. Your journey to becoming a member of the U.S. Armed Forces begins here, with this comprehensive preparation for the ASVAB. Let's embark on this journey together, with determination, focus, and the aspiration to excel.

Unit I. GENERAL SCIENCE (GS)

ey future heroes! Welcome to Unit 1, your gateway to mastering the General Science section of the ASVAB. We'll dive into the captivating worlds of Biology & Anatomy, Earth & Space, and Physics & Chemistry. From the tiny cellular processes that keep us alive to the vast expanse of the universe, this chapter has it all. Grasping these concepts is crucial, not just for the ASVAB, but for your future military career where scientific knowledge can be a game-changer. Don't just cram; truly understand. Picture yourself pulling an all-nighter and hitting the books, but with a strategy that works. Remember, this journey isn't about stress; it's about unlocking your potential and acing this test with confidence. Let's embark on this mission together and nail it on the first try!

BIOLOGY & ANATOMY

Life's Foundations
Cells, Genetics, and Pathogens

Diving right in, we are starting with the very foundations of life itself: Cells, Genetics, and those uninvited guests, the Pathogens. This isn't just a theoretical journey; it's a practical, hands-on exploration of the secrets that define us and the external forces that sometimes challenge our well-being.

Now, I know these terms might sound a bit high-flying, but trust me, we're going to break them down into bite-sized pieces that are easy to digest. Picture this as your all-access pass to the grand theater of life, where you'll learn about the cellular power stations keeping us running, the genetic blueprint that makes us unique, and those tiny invaders that sometimes throw a wrench in the works.

As we gear up to delve deeper, let's strategize a bit. In this segment, you'll be answering about 10 questions, a substantial part of the Biology & Anatomy section. But remember, you've got a full 20 minutes to work through this, so there's no need to rush. Take a moment, breathe, and embrace your inner scientist as we unpack what to anticipate in each of these fascinating areas of study.

Cells

Imagine cells as the Lego pieces of life. They're the tiniest building blocks that come together to create everything – from your skin to your muscles to your brain. We'll discuss cell structure, how they reproduce, and why they're the real MVPs of your body's orchestra.

- **Cell Structure:**
  Picture this, cells are like mini cities, bustling with activity and specialized workers. At the heart of these cities is the nucleus, which is like the city hall containing all the instructions – your DNA! Imagine DNA as a collection of blueprints that dictate everything about you. Then we've got the cytoplasm, the jelly-like substance that hosts various organelles. Think of organelles as your city's departments – the mitochondria are the powerhouses, generating energy like electricity, while the Golgi apparatus packages and ships cellular goodies like Amazon Prime. And don't forget the cell membrane – it's like the city walls, keeping things in and out, and even hosting special doors called receptors to interact with the outside world.

- **Cell Processes:**
  Now, let's hit the play button on the cellular theater. Imagine you're watching a movie where cells carry out processes that keep life moving along. First up, we've got mitosis, the magical duplication act where one cell becomes two identical ones. It's like a cell's version of cloning! Then there's meio-

sis, a special performance that creates eggs and sperm with half the usual number of chromosomes. It's like the ultimate genetic mixtape!

But that's not all – cells also throw a party known as protein synthesis. This is where ribosomes read the DNA's instructions and whip up proteins like master chefs. These proteins do everything from building and repairing tissues to being the architects of your immune system's defense strategies. Now, imagine your cells receiving letters. These letters are hormones, secreted by glands in your endocrine system. They're like messages sent to different parts of the city, coordinating growth, mood, and all sorts of vital functions. Finally, let's talk about cellular respiration, the metabolic magic that converts nutrients into energy. It's like the city's power plant converting fuel into electricity, except the fuel is glucose and the electricity is a molecule called ATP that powers every cell's activity. So, there you have it, fellow explorers – the stunning symphony of cell structure and processes! From the nucleus orchestrating the show to protein factories humming away, cells are the unsung heroes that keep the grand tale of life in motion. Remember, it's not just about memorizing terms; it's about understanding the captivating dance of life at its smallest level. So, keep your curiosity alive and let's keep sailing through the sea of science!"

Genetics

Get ready to explore the DNA dance floor! Genetics is like a cosmic recipe book that determines everything about you. We'll decipher the basics of inheritance, genes, and how those blueprints make you, well, you. From dominant traits to recessive ones, we'll uncover the genetic code that's been passed down through generations.

Pathogens

Brace yourself because we're diving into the world of tiny terrors. Pathogens are those cunning microorganisms that can mess with your health. Viruses, bacteria, fungi – they're the villains in this story. But fear not! We'll show you how your immune system gears up to protect you from these microscopic troublemakers. Remember, this isn't about cramming every tiny detail

into your brain like a storage unit – it's about grasping the concepts, understanding the connections, and seeing how they fit into the grand tapestry of life. So, buckle up, stay curious, and let's conquer Cells, Genetics, and Pathogens together!

Anatomy Overview
Systems, Movement, and Support

Understanding human anatomy is of paramount importance as you prepare for the ASVAB examination. While it might seem unrelated to military service at first glance, knowledge of our body's intricate systems can provide essential insights into numerous operations and situations.

Systems

Imagine your body as a bustling metropolis, and the systems are like the city's departments. You've got the digestive system processing food like a master chef, the respiratory system helping you breathe easy, and the circulatory system acting as the ultimate delivery service, transporting oxygen and nutrients to every corner of your body. We'll break down each system, giving you the inside scoop on how they work and how they come together to keep you in tip-top shape.

A system in anatomy refers to a collection of organs and structures that have a specific purpose or function. Here are the major systems in the human body (Figure 1.1):

- **Digestive System:**
  Responsible for breaking down food so that it can be used by the body. It starts from the mouth and includes the esophagus, stomach, intestines, liver, pancreas, and ends at the rectum.

- **Respiratory System:**
  Takes in oxygen and releases carbon dioxide. It encompasses the nose, trachea, bronchi, and lungs.

- **Cardiovascular/Circulatory System:**
  Circulates blood throughout the body, ensuring oxygen, nutrients, and other essential substances are distributed to cells. It consists of the heart, blood vessels, and blood.

- **Nervous System:**
  Acts as the body's control system and communication network. It includes the brain, spinal cord, nerves, and sense organs.

- **Muscular System:**
  Provides movement, both voluntary and involuntary. It is made up of three types of muscles: skeletal, smooth, and cardiac.

- **Skeletal System:**
  Provides support, protection, and shape to the body. It also produces blood cells and stores minerals. This system is made up of bones, cartilage, and joints.

- **Endocrine System:**
  Consists of glands that produce hormones, which are chemical messengers that regulate various body functions. It includes the thyroid gland, pituitary gland, adrenal glands, and others.

- **Reproductive System:**
  Allows humans to reproduce. In males, it includes structures like the testes and prostate, while in females, it encompasses the ovaries, uterus, and fallopian tubes.

- **Urinary System:**
  Removes waste products from the blood and expels them from the body. It includes the kidneys, bladder, ureters, and urethra.

- **Lymphatic System:**
  Helps defend the body against infections and diseases. It includes the lymph nodes, spleen, thymus, and tonsils.

- **Integumentary System:**
  Protects the body from external harm and includes the skin, hair, nails, and sweat glands.

THE HUMAN BODY
Internal organs

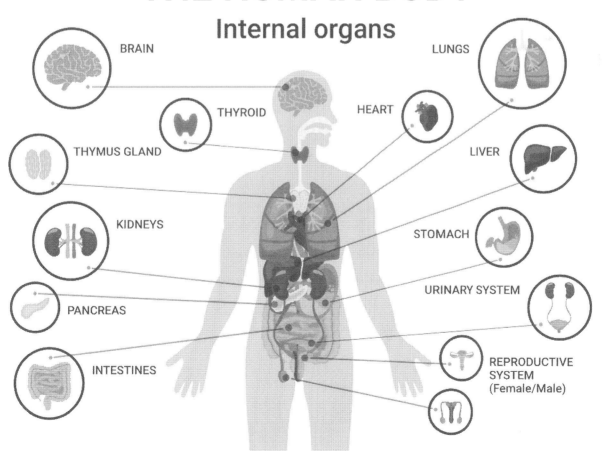

Figure 1.1: Illustration of the internal organs of a human body

Movement

Movement, in the anatomical sense, is the act of changing physical position or location.

The primary system responsible for movement is the Muscular System. It comprises over 600 muscles that, when contracted, allow for various types of movements:

- **Skeletal muscles:**
  Responsible for voluntary movements, like walking or lifting.

- **Smooth muscles:**
  Found in organs and responsible for involuntary movements, like the contraction of the stomach.

- **Cardiac muscle:**
  Found only in the heart and facilitates the heart's beating.

Support

The term "support" refers to structures that maintain the body's shape, provide protection to internal organs, and anchor muscles for movement.

The chief system for this is the Skeletal System. It has 206 bones in adults, which serve multiple purposes:

- **Support:**
  Bones give structure to the body.

- **Protection:**
  Bones like the skull and rib cage safeguard vital organs.

- **Movement:**
  Bones provide leverage for muscles, aiding in movement.

- **Mineral Storage:**
  Bones store minerals, notably calcium and phosphorus.

- **Blood Cell Production:**
  Bone marrow produces red blood cells, white blood cells, and platelets.

Here's a simple table design for "Systems", "Movement", and "Support," showcasing their unique characteristics:

Category	Description	Unique Characteristics
Systems	Refers to the grouped organs in the body which work together to carry out a specific function.	- Digestive system processes food. - Respiratory system manages breathing. - Circulatory system handles blood circulation.
Movement	Relates to the muscular system enabling motion and flexibility.	- Muscles work in pairs (one contracts while the other relaxes). - Provides strength and stamina. - Enables body to respond quickly to stimuli.
Support	Pertains to the skeletal system which provides structure and protection to the body.	- Protects vital organs (e.g., skull protects brain). - Provides structure and posture. - Facilitates movement via joints.

Nature's Network
Ecology and Biodiversity Classification

Nature functions as an intricate web of connections, often referred to as the network of life. At the heart of this network is the study of ecology, which delves into the relationships between organisms and the environments in which they reside. Ecology examines the interactions that determine the distribution, abundance, and well-being of living organisms. It's not just about individual species; it's about ecosystems, communities, and biomes. On the other hand, biodiversity stands as a testament to the variety within this network, encompassing the different species, genetic variations within these species, and the myriad ecosystems they form. Classification of biodiversity becomes paramount in understanding and preserving this diversity.

By categorizing life forms into hierarchical categories such as kingdom, phylum, class, order, family, genus, and species, we can begin to appreciate the vast tapestry of life that our planet sustains. This organized approach is not merely an academic exercise but a crucial tool in conservation, enabling us to pinpoint where our preservation efforts are most needed. The fusion of ecology with the classification of biodiversity provides us with a profound understanding of the delicate balance that sustains life on Earth.

Ecology
Ecology, at its core, is the study of interactions between living organisms and their environment, including both biotic (living) and abiotic (non-living) components. Let's understand this concept using an analogy with the armed forces. Picture the armed forces as a living organism within the larger environment of global geopolitics. The various branches of the military (Army, Navy, Air Force, etc.) can be seen as different 'organs' or subsystems, each with its unique function but all working in harmony to ensure the well-being and security of the nation. The relationships and dependencies between these branches, such as intelligence sharing or joint operations, mimic the interactions between species in an ecosystem.

Now, consider the external factors or 'environmental conditions' in this analogy. Geopolitical issues, like territorial disputes or trade wars, can be likened to abiotic factors in ecology, such as temperature or rainfall, influencing the behavior and strategy of the armed forces. The alliances and treaties with other nations mirror the mutualistic relationships between species in an ecosystem, where both parties benefit from cooperation.

Furthermore, just as an ecosystem can experience disturbances, like fires or droughts, the armed forces might face challenges, be it cyber-attacks or political unrest. The resilience of the armed forces, like the resilience of an ecosystem, depends on its internal structure, diversity, and adaptability. In this analogy, the 'biodiversity' within the armed forces—represented by diverse skills, tactics, equipment, and personnel—is paramount to its overall health and ability to respond to threats. The more versatile and adaptable the force, the better equipped it is to handle challenges, much like an ecosystem with high biodiversity is more resilient to environmental changes.

Biodiversity Classification
Biodiversity classification is the process of categorizing the vast variety of life on Earth based on shared characteristics and genetic ties. This systematic organization allows us to understand and study the immense diversity of life forms more efficiently. At its most basic, biodiversity is classified into three primary levels:

- **Genetic Diversity:**
  Refers to the variations in genes within a species. This is the reason why individuals of the same species, like humans, look different from one another.

- **Species Diversity:**
  Focuses on the variety of species within a particular region. For instance, a tropical rainforest might have more species diversity than a desert.

- **Ecosystem Diversity:**
  Refers to the range of different habitats found within a region, from forests and lakes to deserts and mountains. Each ecosystem has its unique set of species and interactions.

To systematically categorize biodiversity, scientists use a hierarchical method called "taxonomy." Organisms are classified into a series of ranks, starting broadly and becoming more specific. The primary ranks, in descending order of inclusiveness, are: Domain, Kingdom, Phylum, Class, Order, Family, Genus, and Species. Each rank narrows down the classification, culminating in a unique species name (Figure 1.2).

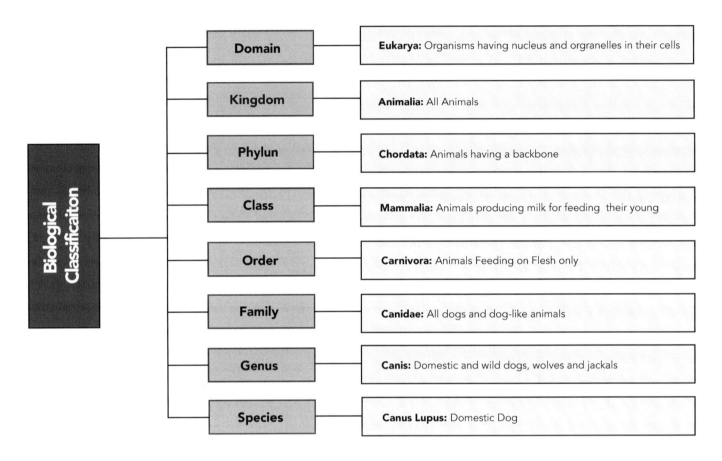

Figure 1.2: Biological classification system

Species

This is the fundamental unit of classification. A species is a group of organisms that can interbreed to produce fertile offspring. It's like a unique club where members share common traits and DNA secrets.

Genus

Genus is a broader category that includes one or more species that are closely related. Think of it as a family surname, grouping similar species together.

Family, Order, Class, Phylum, Kingdom

These are ascending levels of classification, like chapters in a book. Each level groups organisms based on shared characteristics, and the higher you go, the broader the similarities become. From specific species to the broadest categories, these levels help us understand the relationships among all living things.

Convergent Evolution

This is like nature's version of copy-paste. Convergent evolution happens when unrelated species develop similar traits to adapt to similar environments. It's like different brands creating the same cool gadget without knowing the other exists.

Divergent Evolution

Divergent evolution occurs when species with a common ancestor evolve different traits due to varying environments or lifestyles. It's like siblings pursuing different career paths based on their interests.

Adaptive Radiation

Imagine a single species branching out into multiple diverse species to occupy various ecological niches. This is adaptive radiation – one ancestral species giving rise to numerous new species, each adapting to different environments. It's like a single idea sparking a thousand innovations. So, there you have it, fellow explorers – a pocketful of essential terms to guide you through the vast world of biodiversity classification. Remember, these terms aren't just for impressing your friends; they're tools to help you understand the incredible complexity of life on Earth. Now, go forth and conquer the world of taxonomy with your newfound knowledge!

Ecosystems and Interactions:

Now, picture Earth as a cosmic playground, where every organism has its own swing to play on. Ecosystems are these playgrounds – they're like little worlds where plants, animals, and the environment team up to create a delicate balance. Imagine predators and prey engaging in an eternal game of tag, or plants and insects collaborating in a ballet of pollination. It's a dance of life, and every step counts. Let's gear up and explore the thrilling terrain of important terms and concepts that revolve around ecosystems and the captivating interactions within them. Now, get ready to uncover the secrets of nature's playground!

Ecosystem

Think of an ecosystem as a bustling community where living organisms interact with each other and their physical environment. From the tiniest microbe to the mightiest tree, everyone has a role to play in this cosmic drama.

Biotic Factors

Now, think of abiotic factors as the stage itself – the non-living elements that set the scene. Things like temperature, sunlight, soil composition, and water availability create the backdrop for the ecosystem's story.

Abiotic Factors

Now, think of abiotic factors as the stage itself – the non-living elements that set the scene. Things like temperature, sunlight, soil composition, and water availability create the backdrop for the ecosystem's story.

Producers, Consumers, Decomposers

These are the main players in the food web of an ecosystem. Producers (plants) use sunlight to create energy through photosynthesis. Consumers are organisms that eat other organisms – herbivores eat plants, carnivores eat animals, and omnivores indulge in both. Decomposers, like fungi and bacteria, clean up the stage by breaking down dead matter.

Food Chain and Food Web

Picture a string of Christmas lights connecting organisms based on who eats whom. That's a food chain – a linear path of energy flow. But ecosystems are more complex, so we have food webs, which are like intricate mosaics of interconnected food chains. It's like a giant potluck where everyone's connected by who's on the menu.

Energy Pyramid

Imagine energy as the currency of ecosystems. An energy pyramid illustrates how energy decreases as you move up the food chain. Producers have the most energy, but it dwindles with each step to consumers. It's like a budget that gets smaller with each transaction.

Biomes

These are nature's neighborhoods – vast regions with distinct climates, plants, animals, and ecosystems. From the icy tundra to the sweltering deserts, each biome has its own story to tell.

Symbiosis

Symbiosis is the art of teamwork in the wild. There's mutualism, where both species benefit (think bees and flowers); parasitism, where one benefits and the other is harmed (like ticks on animals); and commensalism, where one benefits and the other is neither helped nor harmed (like birds perching on trees).

Predator-Prey Dynamics

Imagine a never-ending game of tag in the wild. Predators are the "taggers," hunting and feeding on prey for survival. But don't feel too bad for the prey – they develop strategies to evade capture, like a gazelle's speed or a rabbit's burrow.

Biodiversity and Our Planet

Here's the grand finale: the deeper we understand biodiversity, the better we can protect it. Imagine being a conservation superhero, ensuring that every species, from the tiniest ant to the mightiest elephant, has a place in Earth's story. Biodiversity isn't just about admiring the variety of life; it's about recognizing that we're all part of this cosmic tapestry, and each thread matters. Let's unravel the intricate threads of Ecology and Biodiversity Classification. It's not just about learning facts; it's about immersing ourselves in the drama of life's theater and understanding our role in this intricate web. Get ready to be amazed, inspired, and above all, to see the world around us with new eyes. Let's set sail on this journey of discovery and be the stewards of our magnificent planet!

Biodiversity

Biodiversity is the spice of life, encompassing the variety of living organisms in an ecosystem. High biodiversity is like a vibrant festival with numerous acts, while low biodiversity is like a solo performance.

So, fellow nature enthusiasts, armed with these terms and concepts, you're now equipped to explore the enchanting world of ecosystems and interactions (Figure 1.3). It's not just about memorizing facts; it's about unraveling the intricate dance of life and understanding how every organism contributes to the grand symphony of nature. Let's lace up our boots, venture into the wilderness, and be amazed by the story's nature has to share!

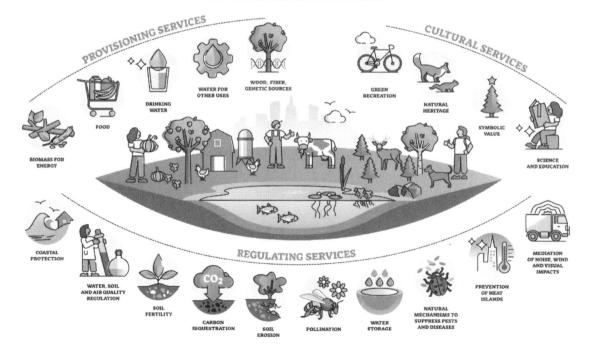

Figure 1.3: Subdivision of Ecological System Services

EARTH & SPACE

Greetings, fellow cosmic travelers! Buckle up for a mind-bending journey as we delve into the Earth & Space section. This is where we'll unravel the secrets of our planet's inner workings and cast our gaze beyond the stars to explore the vast wonders of the universe. Get ready for an adventure that spans from the depths of our planet to the far reaches of outer space!

Dynamic Earth

Imagine Earth as a living, breathing entity. In this section, we'll dig deep into Earth's core, uncovering the molten dance that drives tectonics and fuels volcanoes. It's like peering into the beating heart of our planet, where powerful forces shape the landscape and create the diverse environments we call home.

Atmosphere and Beyond

Look up! That's the vast expanse of the atmosphere, stretching above us like a protective blanket. From the air we breathe to the weather that dances across the sky, we'll unlock the mysteries of Earth's atmospheric wonders. But our exploration doesn't stop there – we'll also venture beyond our atmosphere to explore the boundless realm of outer space.

The Solar System Odyssey

Imagine embarking on a cosmic road trip through our neighborhood in space. We'll journey through the Solar System, visiting planets, moons, and even the enigmatic asteroid belt. It's like exploring a gallery of celestial marvels, each with its own story and unique features.

Stars, Galaxies, and Beyond

Now, let's zoom out to the grand tapestry of the universe. Stars twinkle like cosmic gems, forming constellations that have guided explorers for ages. We'll dive into galaxies, those cosmic cities of stars, and explore phenomena like black holes and nebulae. It's like unlocking the secrets of a vast cosmic encyclopedia.

Space Exploration and Discoveries

Imagine stepping into the shoes of an astronaut, soaring through the cosmos. We'll journey through the history of space exploration, from the first satellites to moon landings and beyond. It's like reliving the moments when humanity reached out and touched the stars.

Cosmic Mysteries and Theories

Picture the universe as a puzzle waiting to be solved. We'll delve into mind-boggling mysteries like dark matter and dark energy – the elusive components that make up most of the cosmos. And let's not forget the mind-bending theories that attempt to explain the nature of space, time, and reality itself.

Astronomy and the Night Sky

Imagine the night sky as a vast canvas splashed with stars. We'll explore the science of astronomy, learning how telescopes reveal the secrets of distant galaxies and planets. It's like embarking on a celestial treasure hunt, discovering hidden wonders in the vast expanse above.

So, fellow adventurers, with the Earth & Space section as our launchpad, we're set to journey through the cosmos like never before. This isn't just about amassing facts; it's about igniting a cosmic curiosity that propels us to explore, question, and marvel at the mysteries that surround us. From the intricate workings of our planet to the mind-boggling vastness of the universe, let's embrace adventure and set our sights on the stars!

Planet Profiles
Geology, Tectonics, and Earth's Timeline

Greetings, cosmic explorers! Get ready to journey through the ages and uncover the ancient tales of our home planet. In this segment, we're diving deep into the heart of Geology, unraveling the mysteries of Tectonics, and taking a ride through Earth's remarkable timeline. Strap in, because we're about to traverse the rocky road of our planet's history!

Geology: Unveiling Earth's Secrets
Imagine Earth as a massive puzzle waiting to be solved. Geology is the ultimate detective work, where we decode the planet's composition, structure, and the forces that have shaped it over eons. It's like peeling back the layers of history written in stone.

- **Rock Types:** Geology starts with rocks – the foundation of our planet. There are three main types: igneous rocks (formed from cooled magma or lava), sedimentary rocks (created from layers of sediment), and metamorphic rocks (altered by heat and pressure). Each rock type holds clues to Earth's history.

- **Minerals:** Imagine rocks as books, and minerals are their words. Minerals are the building blocks of rocks, with distinct properties like color, hardness, and crystal structure. From sparkling quartz to glittering gold, minerals are Earth's dazzling gems.

- **Stratigraphy:** Think of Earth's rock layers as history's pages. Stratigraphy is the study of these layers and their chronological sequence. It's like piecing together the chapters of Earth's story by examining the layers' order and contents.

- **Fossils:** Fossils are like snapshots of ancient life. These preserved remains of plants and animals reveal Earth's biological history. By studying fossils, geologists unlock tales of long-extinct creatures and the environments they inhabited.

- **Plate Tectonics:** The ultimate geological blockbuster. Earth's lithosphere (crust and upper mantle) is divided into tectonic plates that move and interact. This movement creates earthquakes, mountain ranges, and ocean basins – reshaping our planet over time.

- **Volcanism:** Volcanoes are Earth's fiery artists. When molten rock (magma) erupts onto the surface, it forms new landforms and deposits. Volcanic activity also releases gases and influences Earth's climate.

- **Erosion and Weathering:** Geology's sculptors, erosion and weathering, reshape landscapes. Erosion transports rocks and soil through wind, water, and ice, while weathering breaks rocks down through chemical and physical processes.

- **Geological Time:** Geologists are time travellers. The Earth's timeline is divided into eons, eras, periods, and epochs. These divisions help us understand Earth's history, from its fiery birth to the emergence of complex life forms.

- **Geological Maps:** Maps aren't just for navigation; they're a geologist's treasure map. Geological maps display rock formations, faults, and other features, helping us decode Earth's history by studying its surface expressions.

- **Geothermal Energy:** Earth's warmth isn't just a cozy feeling – it's a source of energy. Geothermal energy harnesses heat from within the Earth to generate electricity and provide heating for homes and industries.

- **Geologic Hazards:** Geology has its share of challenges. Earthquakes, landslides, volcanic eruptions, and tsunamis are examples of geologic hazards that affect landscapes and communities.

- **Geologic Record:** Imagine Earth's history as a massive library. The geologic record is this library's shelves, storing evidence of past events. From rock layers to fossils, it's a chronicle of our planet's journey.

So, dear geology enthusiasts, armed with these terms and concepts, you're ready to embark on a geological adventure. Remember, geology isn't just about studying rocks; it's about deciphering Earth's epic story. Whether you're exploring ancient fossils or decoding the secrets of shifting continents, every discovery is a step deeper into our planet's captivating narrative. Get ready to uncover the mysteries that have shaped our world – it's time to rock on!

Tectonics Unveiled: Earth's Shifting Puzzle Pieces

Get ready to journey into the heart of Earth's dynamic dance – the captivating world of tectonics. Imagine our planet as a colossal puzzle, where pieces of Earth's crust, known as tectonic plates, shift, collide, and reshape the landscape. Welcome to the mesmerizing realm of tectonics, where continents drift and mountains rise in a geological symphony.

- **Plate Boundaries:** Think of tectonic plate boundaries as the stage where Earth's drama unfolds. There are three main types: divergent boundaries (plates move apart, creating mid-ocean ridges), convergent boundaries (plates collide, forming mountains and deep ocean trenches), and transform boundaries (plates slide past each other, causing earthquakes along faults).

- **Continental Drift:** Imagine Earth's continents as nomads on a grand journey. The theory of continental drift suggests that continents were once part of a supercontinent called Pangaea. Over eons, Pangaea broke apart, and the continents migrated to their current positions, fitting like pieces of a cosmic puzzle.

- **Seafloor Spreading:** Dive beneath the oceans to discover seafloor spreading – a phenomenon that occurs at divergent boundaries. Here, magma rises from the mantle, creating new seafloor as plates pull apart. As the magma cools and solidifies, it leaves behind magnetic stripes that offer a glimpse into Earth's magnetic history.

- **Subduction Zones:** Imagine one plate descending beneath another – that's subduction. At convergent boundaries, oceanic plates dive into the mantle, forming deep ocean trenches. These subduction zones are not only responsible for creating volcanic arcs but also for recycling Earth's crust.

- **Plate Tectonics and Earthquakes:** Picture the tension building along a fault line – a boundary where tectonic plates meet. Suddenly, the tension releases, causing an earthquake. These seismic events offer a window into the dynamic forces at play within Earth's crust.

- **Volcanic Activity:** Volcanic eruptions are the result of tectonic action. At subduction zones, melting oceanic plates generate magma that rises to the surface, creating explosive volcanoes. Meanwhile, at divergent boundaries, magma from the mantle creates new landforms and seafloor.

- **Mountain Building:** Tectonics are the architects of Earth's mountains. At convergent boundaries, immense pressure and folding uplift Earth's crust, giving birth to majestic mountain ranges. The Himalayas and the Andes are prime examples of tectonics sculpting Earth's majestic peaks.

- **Tectonics and Landscapes:** From the rugged Alps to the serene Grand Canyon, tectonics shape Earth's diverse landscapes. The movement of tectonic plates molds valleys, lifts mountains, and carves coastlines, creating the breathtaking vistas that define our world.

Given below are the principal tectonic plates on Earth:

- North American Plate
- Pacific Plate
- Cocos Plate
- Caribbean Plate
- Nazca Plate
- Juan de Fuca Plate
- South American Plate

- Scotia Plate
- Eurasian Plate
- Arabian Plate
- African Plate
- Somali Plate
- Antarctic Plate
- Indian Plate
- Australian Plate
- Philippine Plate

So, there you have it, explorers of Earth's puzzle – an introduction to the captivating world of tectonics. This is more than just geological jargon; it's the story of Earth's ever-changing face. Tectonics reveal the power, beauty, and constant motion that define our planet. As you delve into this world, remember that beneath our feet lies a dynamic landscape where puzzle pieces shift and mountains rise. Get ready to witness the tectonic forces that have shaped our world's magnificent tapestry!

Earth's Timeline Unveiled: A Journey Through Millennia
Step into the time machine of geology as we uncover Earth's remarkable history – a narrative that spans billions of years and holds the secrets of our planet's evolution. Imagine flipping through the pages of time, witnessing the birth of continents, the rise of life, and the epic events that have shaped Earth into the world we know today (Figure 1.4).

- **Hadean Eon:** Picture Earth in its infancy, a world of chaos and heat. This is the Hadean Eon, marked by intense volcanic activity, meteor bombardments, and the formation of our young planet's crust. It offers a glimpse into the fiery birth of Earth.

- **Archean Eon:** Journey further back to the Archean Eon. Envision a young Earth with forming oceans and the emergence of simple life. The Archean marks the earliest signs of life, with ancient microorganisms thriving in Earth's oceans.

- **Proterozoic** Eon: See Earth transform into a recognizable world – continents forming, oceans expanding, and life diversifying. The Proterozoic Eon showcases the emergence of complex cells, setting the stage for an explosion of life.

- **Paleozoic Era:** Enter a world where ancient oceans teemed with life and the first animals ventured onto land. The Paleozoic Era introduces the rise of fish, amphibians, reptiles, and the iconic age of early reptiles.

- **Mesozoic Era:** Picture the Mesozoic Era as the reign of the dinosaurs – a time when Earth's landscapes were dominated by colossal reptiles. Dinosaurs evolved, birds took to the skies, and flowering plants began to flourish.

- **Cenozoic Era:** Imagine the past million years, where mammals took center stage after the dinosaurs' dramatic exit. The Cenozoic Era brings us closer to familiar times, with the emergence of primates, mammals, and eventually, humans.

- **Quaternary Period:** In the blink of geological time, we arrive at the Quaternary Period – the era of ice ages and the rise of Homo sapiens. Imagine woolly mammoths roaming icy landscapes and early humans crafting tools and mastering fire.

- **Modern Times:** Finally, envision the world we inhabit today. Our modern era is marked by the impact of human activity on the planet. From the Industrial Revolution to the technological age, humans have become a significant geological force, shaping landscapes and ecosystems.

GEOLOGIC TIMELINE

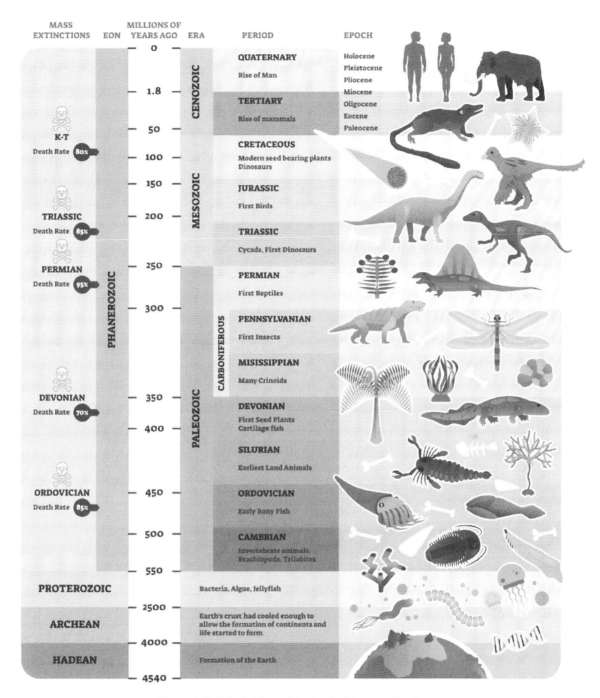

Figure 1.3: Subdivision of Ecological System Services

So, there you have it, time travellers of geology – a glimpse into Earth's vast timeline. It's a saga that began with fiery beginnings, saw the rise of life, witnessed the reign of ancient giants, and eventually led to the dawn of humanity. As you explore Earth's timeline, remember that each era holds its own unique tales, from the simplest microorganisms to the complex societies of today. Get ready to traverse through epochs and eons, witnessing the grand story of our planet's journey through time!

As we conclude our expedition through the pages of "Planet Profiles: Geology, Tectonics, and Earth's Timeline," we stand in awe of the geological wonders that have shaped our world. From the fiery birth of Earth's crust to the majestic dance of tectonic plates, and the epic tale of our planet's journey through time, we've delved deep into the heart of Earth's geological story.

We've marvelled at the intricate layers of rocks that hold the whispers of ancient landscapes. We've witnessed the raw power of volcanic eruptions, the grandeur of mountain ranges forged by tectonic forces, and the delicate imprints of fossils that reveal Earth's rich history. We've journeyed through epochs and eons, from the emergence of life in ancient oceans to the dominance of dinosaurs and the rise of modern humanity.

Throughout this exploration, we've uncovered the threads that bind Earth's geology, tectonics, and timeline together – a captivating narrative of constant change, incredible forces, and the resilience of life. We've walked in the footsteps of pioneers who decoded Earth's mysteries and ventured into the unknown to unravel its secrets.

As we close this chapter, let us remember that the Earth's geology is not just a story of the past; it's a living, breathing tale that continues to shape our present and future. The forces that shaped mountains and carved valleys are still at work, reminding us of the dynamic nature of our planet. From the rocky landscapes to the shifting tectonic plates, every layer of Earth's story is a testament to its enduring beauty and complexity.

So, fellow explorers, as you turn the final page of "Planet Profiles: Geology, Tectonics, and Earth's Timeline," carry with you the wonder and wisdom that this journey has bestowed upon you. Whether you're gazing at a majestic mountain range or feeling the tremors of an earthquake, may you see the Earth's geological tapestry with newfound appreciation and curiosity. Let the echoes of Earth's geological symphony inspire you to keep exploring, keep questioning, and keep marvelling at the marvels of our incredible planet.

Weather & Sky
Atmospheric Sciences and Celestial Explorations

Welcome, fellow sky gazers and weather enthusiasts, to a celestial journey where we'll unravel the mysteries of the heavens and decode the secrets of Earth's ever-changing atmosphere. In this chapter, we'll embark on a quest to understand the delicate dance of clouds, the drama of storms, and the cosmic wonders that adorn our night skies. So, fellow cosmic travelers, as we dive into "Weather & Sky: Atmospheric Sciences and Celestial Explorations," be prepared to unravel the atmospheric mysteries that shape our world and gaze upon the celestial wonders that ignite our imaginations. Whether you're a cloud whisperer, a stargazing dreamer, or simply curious about the universe, this chapter invites you to embrace the magic that unfolds both above and around us. Let's set sail on this journey, where the sky's the limit, and the weather is just the beginning!

Atmospheric Marvels:

Imagine the air around you as a canvas painted with stories of weather and climate. Atmospheric sciences delve into this realm, studying the layers that envelop our planet. From the troposphere, where weather unfolds, to the stratosphere, where jet streams dance, we'll explore the intricate threads that shape our daily lives.

In this context, "Atmospheric Marvels" refers to the fascinating and complex phenomena that occur within Earth's atmosphere. Think of the atmosphere as a vast theater where weather, climate, and various processes interact. The atmospheric sciences are like the scriptwriters and directors who study and understand these processes. The different layers of the atmosphere, like the troposphere (where weather occurs) and the stratosphere (where jet streams flow), are like different scenes in this grand production. This section promises to take readers on a journey through these atmospheric layers, uncovering the wonders and mysteries they hold.

Weather Patterns:

Prepare for the meteorological rollercoaster of weather patterns. Picture warm air rising, cool air sinking, and the choreography of high and low-pressure systems. These patterns orchestrate everything from gentle breezes to fierce storms.

"Weather Patterns" refers to the regular and repeated atmospheric conditions and behaviors that we observe. Just like a choreographed dance, these patterns involve the movement of air masses, changes in temperature, pressure systems, and other atmospheric phenomena. Warm air rising and cool air sinking create air currents that influence weather. High and low-pressure systems are like the main actors in this atmospheric drama, determining whether you'll experience a sunny day or a rainy one. This section promises to explain the science behind these patterns and how they influence our daily weather.

Cloud Symphony:

Look up and witness the ever-changing spectacle of clouds. From fluffy cumulus clouds that resemble cotton candy to the mighty cumulonimbus clouds that signal thunderstorms, clouds tell stories across the sky. We'll explore how temperature, humidity, and air currents create these formations.

"Cloud Symphony" is a metaphorical way of describing the visual beauty and dynamic nature of clouds in the sky. Just like a symphony is a harmonious arrangement of musical notes, clouds create a captivating visual composition. Different types of clouds, like cumulus and cumulonimbus, are like various instruments playing their part. The mention of temperature, humidity, and air currents emphasizes that cloud formation is a result of intricate interactions in the atmosphere. This section promises to take readers on a journey to understand cloud types, their formations, and how they contribute to the ever-changing canvas of the sky.

Stormy Encounters:

Storms are the dramatic performances of weather – powerful and commanding. Thunderstorms, hurricanes, and tornadoes are the rockstars of meteorology. We'll uncover their origins, examine their destructive power, and appreciate the awe-inspiring beauty of lightning and thunder.

"Stormy Encounters" paints a vivid picture of the intense and dramatic nature of storms. Just as encounters with rockstars are memorable and attention-grabbing, encounters with storms are powerful and unforgettable. Thunderstorms, hurricanes, and tornadoes are highlighted as the most dynamic and attention-worthy aspects of meteorology. This section promises to explain the science behind these storms, exploring how they form, their potential for destruction, and the mesmerizing natural phenomena they bring, like lightning and thunder.

PHYSICS & CHEMISTRY

Welcome to a realm where the laws of the universe shape the very fabric of reality. In this section, we delve into the intricate relationship between physics and chemistry, two pillars that underpin the natural world. Prepare to uncover the fundamental forces that govern everything from the tiniest atom to the vastness of space, and explore the mesmerizing dance of atoms and molecules that brings the world around us to life.

Physics
The Universe in Motion

Imagine the universe as a cosmic stage, with physics as the choreographer orchestrating its dance. Physics unravels the mysteries of motion, energy, and forces that shape the very foundations of reality. From the delicate balance of gravity to the dazzling dance of light, we'll explore the laws that govern our world and the cosmos beyond.

So, fellow cosmic explorers, as we dive into the next sections, prepare to witness the laws that govern the universe's movements and interactions. From the majestic sweep of planets to the intricate realm of particles, physics unveils a world where principles guide the dance of reality itself. Whether you're pondering the mysteries of a falling apple or marveling at the curvature of spacetime, this journey promises to awaken your curiosity and deepen your understanding of the cosmic stage we call home. Let's venture forth and experience the elegance of the universe's choreography, guided by the laws that shape our existence.

Physics Primer
Mechanics, Energy, and Wave Dynamics

Welcome to a journey through the intricate tapestry of the physical world, where the laws of motion, the dance of energy, and the symphony of waves come together to shape the very essence of reality. In this section, we embark on a quest to understand the mechanics that govern motion, the transformations that fuel the universe, and the mesmerizing oscillations that define our perception of the world.

Unveiling Mechanics: Decoding the Dance of Motion

Picture a world in motion – from the flutter of leaves in the wind to the majestic orbits of planets around the Sun. Mechanics is the science that reveals the principles governing this intricate dance of motion. It's like peeking behind the curtain of reality to understand how objects move, why they behave the way they do, and what rules govern their interactions.

- **Language of Motion:** Imagine a theater where everything moves. Mechanics provides the vocabulary to describe this motion. Terms like velocity, which captures both speed and direction, and acceleration, the rate of change of velocity, become our linguistic tools to make sense of the dynamic world around us.

- **Newton's Laws:** Now, imagine a spotlight illuminating Sir Isaac Newton, the mastermind who unraveled the rules of motion. His three laws are the pillars of classical mechanics. The first law, the law of inertia, reveals that objects remain at rest or in motion unless acted upon by an external force. The

second law establishes the famous equation, force equals mass times acceleration $(F = ma)$, tying together the concepts of force, mass, and acceleration. And the third law introduces the concept of action and reaction – every action has an equal and opposite reaction.

- **Gravity's Grasp:** Let's zoom out to the cosmos. Newton's law of universal gravitation takes center stage. Imagine every object with mass reaching out, creating an invisible web that tugs at everything else. This force, known as gravity, is what keeps our feet on the ground, planets in orbit, and is responsible for the ebb and flow of tides.

- **Harmony of Motion:** Mechanics is the sheet music that orchestrates the grand symphony of motion in the universe. Whether it's the trajectory of a soaring eagle, the gentle swaying of a pendulum, or the complex movements of gears in a clock, mechanics unveils the hidden choreography that defines our reality.

So, as you journey deeper into the realm of mechanics, imagine you're donning the glasses of a physicist, seeing the world not just as it is, but as a harmonious dance of forces, masses, and movements. From the mundane to the magnificent, mechanics is the key that unlocks the secrets of how the world around us twirls, leaps, and glides through the stage of existence.

Energy: The Dynamic Force of Nature

Energy is the driving force that fuels every movement, change, and transformation in the universe. It's the spark that sets the world in motion, from the simplest activities of our daily lives to the cosmic events that shape galaxies. Think of energy as the ultimate player in the grand symphony of existence, enabling every action, from a falling leaf to the combustion engine that propels vehicles.

- **Forms of Energy:** Energy manifests in various forms, each playing a unique role in the intricate dance of the cosmos. Kinetic energy is the energy of motion – imagine a bullet hurtling through the air or the flutter of a bird's wings. Potential energy, on the other hand, is stored energy, waiting for the right moment to be unleashed – think of a stretched rubber band ready to snap or a rock perched on the edge of a cliff.

- **Conservation of Energy:** One of the universe's most profound laws is the conservation of energy. This principle dictates that energy cannot be created or destroyed – it merely changes from one form to another. Picture a pendulum swinging back and forth – as it reaches its highest point, kinetic energy transforms into potential energy, and vice versa. This law underscores the elegant balance that governs energy's behavior.

- **Transfers and Transformations:** Energy is a traveler, shifting from place to place and form to form. Imagine a game of pool – as one ball strikes another, the energy transfers, causing the second ball to move. This interplay of energy fuels the machinery of the universe, from the beating of your heart to the eruption of a volcano.

- **Units of Measurement:** To quantify energy, we use units like the Joule, named after the English physicist James Prescott Joule. A Joule represents a specific amount of energy, often visualized as the energy needed to lift a small apple a short distance off the ground. Additionally, you might encounter calories, a unit commonly used to measure the energy content of food.

- **Energy's Omnipresence:** Energy's influence knows no bounds. It's the warmth of sunlight on your skin, the electricity powering your devices, and the fuel that propels rockets into space. This force permeates every aspect of the universe, from the molecular reactions within your body to the astronomical phenomena occurring light-years away.

- **Harnessing and Understanding:** The study of energy isn't just a theoretical pursuit; it's a foundation for innovation and progress. Understanding energy enables us to design more efficient machines, develop sustainable energy sources, and unravel the mysteries of the cosmos. As you delve into the intricacies of energy, you're unraveling the very fabric of the universe's workings, discovering the threads that tie all things together in a continuous dance of transformation and motion.

Chemical Chronicles
Elements, Bonds, and Transformations

Welcome to the enthralling world of chemistry, where the building blocks of the universe are transformed, combined, and rearranged to create the myriad substances that surround us. In this section, we delve into the tales of elements, the stories of bonds that hold matter together, and the epic narratives of transformations that shape our reality.

Imagine a realm where substances morph, molecules collide, and new compounds emerge. Chemistry is the narrative that explains these changes, the science that explores how atoms unite to form molecules, how molecules interact to create compounds, and how matter undergoes enchanting metamorphoses. As we journey through the Chemical Chronicles, we'll witness the alchemical dance of atoms, the hidden connections that bind them, and the magical art of turning one substance into another.

From the periodic table, where elements find their place, to the bonds that lock atoms in an embrace, this section invites you to explore the symphony of chemistry that plays a vital role in shaping our world. Whether you're an aspiring chemist, a curious explorer, or simply someone fascinated by the magic of transformation, these chronicles promise to unlock the secrets of matter's dance, revealing the scientific stories that underpin our tangible reality. So, let's embark on this alchemical adventure, where elements, bonds, and transformations are the threads that weave the captivating tale of chemistry.

Elements: The Fundamental Bricks of Matter

Imagine a realm where matter is broken down to its most basic constituents – a world where everything is built from a unique set of building blocks. These building blocks are known as elements, the foundational ingredients that make up everything around us. Think of elements as the alphabet of the universe, where every substance, from the air we breathe to the stars in the sky, is composed of a combination of these fundamental characters.

- **Atomic Essence:** Envision elements as the purest forms of matter, each characterized by a specific type of atom. Atoms are the indivisible particles that constitute elements, and each element has its own unique properties, such as its atomic number and atomic mass. Hydrogen, the lightest and most abundant element, has only one proton in its nucleus, while heavier elements like gold have many more.

- **Periodic Table:** Now, imagine organizing elements into a grand arrangement that showcases their relationships. This is the periodic table, a masterpiece of chemistry. Elements are grouped by shared properties, forming families that reveal patterns in behavior. From the noble gases that resist chemical reactions to the reactive alkali metals, the periodic table offers a visual map of the elements' diversity.

- **Chemical Identity:** Picture the identity of substances linked to the elements they contain. Water, for example, is composed of two hydrogen atoms and one oxygen atom – H_2O. Carbon, the backbone of organic compounds, forms the basis of life's molecular structures. Each element brings its distinct characteristics to the compounds it forms, giving rise to the complexity and diversity of the material world.

- **Elemental Interactions:** Envision elements as the players in a grand chemical orchestra. Elements combine to create compounds through chemical reactions, a process where atoms rearrange and bond with each other. Whether it's the fusion of hydrogen in stars, the bonding of oxygen and carbon in carbohydrates, or the complex arrangements of DNA's nitrogenous bases, elements' interactions drive the complexity of matter.

- **The Alchemist's Palette:** Imagine elements as the palette of the universe's painter. They're the colors that blend to create the breathtaking variety of substances around us. From the gaseous hydrogen in stars to the metals that form the Earth's crust, elements compose a symphony of matter that both scientists and artists can marvel at.

So, as you explore the concept of elements, envision yourself peering into the very essence of matter. Each element is like a unique note in the universe's symphony, contributing to the harmonious composition that forms our world. By understanding the characteristics, relationships, and roles of elements, you're delving into the heart of chemistry, uncovering the secrets of the atomic ingredients that make the world tick.

Bonds: The Molecular Connections That Shape Matter

Imagine a world where atoms reach out to each other, forming intricate handshakes that bind them together in unique arrangements. These connections, known as chemical bonds, are the glue that holds molecules and compounds together, creating the diverse structures that make up the substances around us. Think of bonds as the unseen threads that weave the fabric of matter, dictating its properties, behaviors, and transformations.

- **Atomic Handshakes:** Envision atoms as individuals seeking companionship in the vast realm of chemistry. Chemical bonds are the interactions that atoms engage in to achieve a more stable and balanced state. These bonds involve the sharing, giving, or receiving of electrons, the charged particles that orbit an atom's nucleus.

- **Covalent Bonds:** Picture atoms sharing electrons in a cosmic partnership – this is the essence of covalent bonds. When atoms share one or more pairs of electrons, they create molecules. Imagine oxygen molecules forming in the air around you, where two oxygen atoms share two electrons each, resulting in a stable molecule.

- **Ionic Bonds:** Now, imagine atoms parting ways with their electrons, resulting in charged particles called ions. Ionic bonds are the result of the attractive forces between positively charged ions (cations) and negatively charged ions (anions). Picture sodium and chlorine ions coming together to form sodium chloride, better known as table salt.

- **Hydrogen Bonds:** Picture a special kind of interaction, a hydrogen bond, that occurs when a hydrogen atom is shared between two electronegative atoms. This bond, weaker than covalent or ionic bonds, plays a vital role in the structure of biological molecules like DNA and the properties of water.

- **Bond Strength and Stability:** Envision bonds as varying in strength. Covalent bonds are strong, requiring a substantial amount of energy to break, while ionic bonds and hydrogen bonds are comparatively weaker. The strength of a bond influences the stability of molecules and compounds.

- **Transforming Matter:** Imagine bonds as the puppeteers of chemical reactions. When bonds are broken and formed, substances transform, creating new compounds with distinct properties. This dance of rearranging atoms and electrons is at the heart of the chemical reactions that shape our world.

Transformations: The Metamorphosis of Matter

Imagine a world where substances shift and change, undergoing captivating metamorphoses that shape the very fabric of reality. These mesmerizing transitions, known as chemical transformations, are the captivating processes through which matter rearranges itself, creating new substances with distinct properties. Think of transformations as the alchemical magic that turns one substance into another, unveiling the mysteries of matter's ever-changing dance.

- **Atomic Choreography:** Envision atoms as dancers in this cosmic ballet. Chemical transformations involve the rearrangement of atoms and their bonds to create entirely new arrangements. Just as a choreographer arranges dancers in intricate patterns, atoms form different compounds in orchestrated sequences.

- **Reactants to Products:** Imagine substances at the beginning of a chemical reaction, called reactants, as the ingredients ready for transformation. As the reaction progresses, these reactants come together, break their bonds, and rearrange themselves to form new substances – the products of the reaction. This dance of atoms mirrors the creation of compounds that shape the world.

- **Exothermic and Endothermic:** Picture transformations accompanied by energy changes. Some reactions release energy in the form of heat, light, or sound – these are exothermic reactions. On the other hand, endothermic reactions absorb energy from their surroundings, causing a cooling effect. Think of exothermic reactions as the universe giving off energy and endothermic reactions as the universe absorbing energy.

- **Equilibrium:** Now, imagine a chemical dance that doesn't stop – this is a reversible reaction. In reversible reactions, reactants can form products, but products can also revert back to reactants. Eventually, a state of equilibrium is reached, where the rates of the forward and reverse reactions are equal. Picture it as a dynamic balance where the dance continues, but neither side gains the upper hand.

- **Catalysts and Rate:** Envision chemical reactions as performers on a stage, each with its own pace. Catalysts are substances that speed up reactions without being consumed themselves. They're like backstage directors, ensuring the dance proceeds smoothly. Reaction rates, on the other hand, measure how quickly reactants turn into products, influenced by factors like temperature, concentration, and catalysts.

- **Nature's Symphony:** Imagine transformations as the symphony of nature, playing in the background of our existence. From the combustion of fuels that powers engines to the biochemical reactions within your body that sustain life, transformations are the fundamental processes that shape our world.

As you dive into the concept of transformations, envision yourself as a spectator of the universe's grand theater. Each chemical reaction is a scene, each atom a dancer, and each product a new chapter in the story of matter. By understanding transformations, you're decoding the script of the cosmic play, unraveling the processes that shape substances and drive the ever-evolving tapestry of existence.

So, as you explore the concept of bonds, imagine yourself as a witness to the intricate handshakes that atoms share, creating the remarkable structures and behaviors of the material world. Bonds are the keys to understanding why substances behave the way they do, from the simple interactions of water to the complex interplay of molecules in living organisms. By grasping the significance of bonds, you're uncovering the molecular language that governs the building blocks of our universe.

The Final Salute

Congratulations future heroes! You've just conquered the world of General Science, mastering everything from cellular processes to the vast expanses of space. Your hard work and dedication have set the stage for success. Remember, understanding these concepts is not just for the test but for your future military career and beyond. Drive on and keep this momentum!

What We've Achieved

In this chapter, we've journeyed through the fascinating realms of Biology, Anatomy, Ecology, and Earth & Space. We've broken down complex cellular structures, unraveled genetic mysteries, and explored the microscopic battles against pathogens. Our adventure took us through Earth's dynamic processes and the cosmic wonders of the universe. Each concept has built a solid foundation of scientific knowledge, preparing you not just for the ASVAB, but for a future filled with informed decisions and critical thinking.

Why This Matters

Mastering these scientific principles isn't just about acing the ASVAB. It's about equipping yourself with knowledge that applies to real-world situations, both in and out of the military. Whether you're planning missions, solving problems, or making everyday decisions, these skills are invaluable. They're the building blocks of strategic thinking and effective leadership.

John's Final Words of Wisdom

- **Practice Makes Permanent:** Keep reviewing and applying what you've learned. Consistency is key.

- **Context is King:** Understand how these concepts fit into the bigger picture of your military and personal life.

- **Never Stop Learning:** Stay curious and keep expanding your knowledge. It's a lifelong journey.

- **Stay Motivated:** Remember why you started this journey and keep pushing forward with confidence.

You've got this! Let's keep hitting the books and nailing those goals!

Unit II. ARITHMETIC REASONING (AR)

Step into the domain where numbers take on new dimensions and mathematical puzzles become pathways to success. In the Arithmetic Reasoning section of the ASVAB, you're about to embark on a journey that merges numerical prowess with logical thinking. Imagine this section as a testing ground for your ability to decipher and solve real-world scenarios through arithmetic. With a set number of questions and a defined time frame, this segment challenges your agility in tackling mathematical challenges under pressure. As you enter this arena, envision yourself as a mathematical detective, uncovering insights and solutions as you navigate the intricacies of arithmetic reasoning. Embrace the challenge with confidence, knowing that each question is an opportunity to demonstrate your skills and sharpen your analytical abilities. Remember, persistence and practice are key, and with each problem you solve, you are one step closer to mastering the art of arithmetic reasoning.

ARITHMETIC FUNDAMENTALS

Arithmetic
The Language and Landscape of Mathematics

Imagine mathematics as a magnificent edifice, with arithmetic as its solid foundation. In this realm, the fundamentals of arithmetic stand as the sturdy building blocks that support the entire mathematical structure. Picture arithmetic as the language of numbers, operations, and relationships, allowing you to navigate the mathematical landscape with confidence and precision.

- **Numbers:**
  Envision numbers as the stars in the mathematical cosmos. They come in various forms—whole numbers, fractions, decimals—each representing a quantity or value. Just as stars light up the night sky, numbers illuminate the realm of mathematics.

- **Operations:**
  Now, picture operations as the tools that transform numbers. Addition, subtraction, multiplication, and division are the key players in this mathematical toolkit. Imagine addition as the act of bringing numbers together, subtraction as the art of taking away, multiplication as repeated addition, and division as sharing or grouping.

- **Order of Operations:**
  Envision arithmetic as a symphony, where the order of notes matters. The order of operations guides how calculations are performed, ensuring consistent results. The acronym "PEMDAS" (Parentheses, Exponents, Multiplication and Division, Addition and Subtraction) helps you remember the sequence.

- **Fractions and Decimals:**
  Imagine fractions as slices of a mathematical pie, representing parts of a whole. Decimals, on the other hand, are like a numerical point where the whole is divided into tenths, hundredths, and beyond. Visualize these concepts as tools for representing quantities in different ways.

- **Place Value:**
  Picture numbers as guests at a mathematical banquet, each seated according to its value. Place value determines the importance of each digit within a number. Imagine a number like 3,492—the "3" holds thousands, the "4" represents hundreds, and so on.

- **Ratios and Proportions:**
  Envision ratios as the relationships between quantities. A ratio compares two or more numbers, often using the ":" symbol. Proportions, then, are equal

ratios—think of them as the mathematical harmony that maintains balance in various scenarios.

- *Percentages:*
  Picture percentages as the universal language of relative quantities. They express a fraction of 100 and are often used to describe proportions or show how parts relate to the whole.

As you navigate the realm of arithmetic, imagine yourself as an explorer in the world of numbers and operations. The fundamentals of arithmetic are your compass, guiding you through the mathematical landscape with clarity and purpose. By mastering these foundational concepts, you're not only building a solid mathematical foundation but also equipping yourself with the tools to unravel the intricacies of more advanced mathematical concepts in the future.

Numerical Basics
Definitions and Prime Relationships

Imagine numbers as the ancient language of the universe, and in this section, we're delving into the very alphabet of that language. Welcome to Numerical Basics, where we'll uncover the definitions of key numerical terms and explore the mysterious world of prime relationships. Consider this your initiation into the realm of numbers, a journey that will equip you with the understanding to decipher the numerical code that underpins the fabric of our mathematical universe.

- *Numbers Unveiled:*
  Envision numbers as the essence of quantity, a concept as old as time itself. Whole numbers, decimals, fractions—these are the vehicles through which we quantify the world around us. Just as words compose sentences, numbers form the foundation of mathematics.

- *Prime and Composite:*
  Imagine numbers as personalities, each with their own traits. Prime numbers, like stars in the mathematical sky, are indivisible by any number other than themselves and 1. Composite numbers, on the other hand, are like puzzle pieces made up of prime factors. Picture 7 as a prime, while 12 is composite, built from the prime factors 2 and 3.

- *Factors and Multiples:*
  Picture numbers as a web of connections. Factors are the numbers that divide into another number without leaving a remainder. Imagine factors as the building blocks of a number, while multiples are the products of a number and other whole numbers. Visualize 6 as having factors 1, 2, 3, and 6, with multiples like 12 and 18.

- *Primes and Relativity:*
  Envision prime numbers as mathematical loners, standing apart from the crowd. Their unique properties make them intriguing subjects of study. Yet, they're essential in the grand scheme of numbers, forming the basis of many mathematical concepts, including cryptography.

- *Greatest Common Divisor (GCD) and Least Common Multiple (LCM):*
  Imagine the GCD as the peacemaker, finding the largest number that divides two or more numbers without a remainder. The LCM, on the other hand, is the party planner, determining the smallest number that is a multiple of two or more numbers. Picture them as tools to solve real-world problems like scheduling or recipe adjustments.

- *Understanding Relationships:*
  Visualize numbers as characters in an intricate story. They relate to one another in ways that provide insights into the world of mathematics. As you explore these numerical relationships, you're not only unlocking the secrets of numbers but also honing your problem-solving skills.

As you immerse yourself in Numerical Basics, envision yourself as an archeologist unearthing the roots of mathematical language. Every definition and relationship are like pieces of the puzzle, contributing to the bigger picture of numerical understanding. By grasping these fundamentals, you're embracing the building blocks of mathematics, the language of logic that enables you to explore the mathematical universe with insight and confidence.

Fractional Flights
Venturing through Fractions and Decimals

Hey there, ace pilot! So, you're back for more wisdom, eh? Fantastic. We're about to journey through the often-turbulent skies of fractions and decimals, but don't worry. I'll be your co-pilot on this mission.

You see, whether you're eyeballing fuel ratios or calculating the precise angle for a descent, fractions and decimals will show up in your life—military or civilian—like a drill sergeant at 0500. Yep, you can't escape them. But the good news? You can master them. Let's break it down, shall we?

Fraction Fundamentals: Your Training Wheels
Fractions are just one way to talk about parts of a whole. If you've got one apple out of a bag of four, you've got 1/4 of the bag. Simple, right?

Tip #1: Fraction Flip-Flop
Simplifying Like a Pro
Ever see fractions like 4/8? Cut it down to size! Divide the top and bottom by their greatest common divisor—in this case, 4. Boom, you got 1/2. Simplifying makes life easier; trust me on this one.

Tip #2: The Brotherly Swap
Converting Fractions to Decimals
Let's say you got a fraction, like 1/4. Want to make it a decimal? Just divide the numerator by the denominator. So, 1 divided by 4 gives you 0.25. It's like translating military jargon to civilian speak.

Decimal Drill: Stepping Up Your Game
Decimals are just another way to talk about fractions. If fractions are like following a compass, decimals are like using GPS—more modern and sometimes more convenient.

Tip #1: Beware the Never-ending Story
Limit the Digits
Ever bump into decimals that just won't quit? Like 0.666666...? Don't let it mess with you; just round it off to where it makes sense, like 0.67.

Tip #2: Quick-Step Conversion
Decimals Back to Fractions
So, you've got a decimal like 0.25 and want it back in fraction form? Easy. Count the digits after the decimal—that's 2. So, your decimal becomes 25/100, and when simplified, that's 1/4. Boom!

John's Aerial Maneuvers: Sky-High Tips and Tricks

- **Precision Matters:** In the military, a tiny mistake can be disastrous. The same goes for fractions and decimals. A wrong decimal point can turn 10 jets into 100. Always double-check your work.

- **Trust but Verify:** When converting between fractions and decimals, go ahead and double-check with a calculator. In the field, we don't guess; we confirm.

- **Game the System:** Get yourself some fraction and decimal games—yes, they exist. Just like in combat, hands-on practice is the best kind.

Mission Complete
Well, look at you, hotshot! You're now equipped to tackle fractions and decimals like a pro. Remember, math isn't about being a genius; it's about understanding your tools and how to use them.

Exponential Elevations
Power Tools and Math Protocols

Ahoy, mathstronauts! Buckle up because today we're gonna break through the stratosphere and head straight into the cosmic world of exponents. Why "cosmic," you ask? Because, my friends, exponents can take you from the microscopic to the astronomical faster than you can say "rocket fuel"!

I see some of you squirming at the mention of exponents. No worries, mate. We've all been there staring at those tiny numbers floating in the air, wondering if they're friend or foe. Well, consider this your definitive guide to turning those exponents into allies and dominating them like a SEAL does an obstacle course.

Scaling the Exponential Mountain: The Hacks

Exponents, like any elite unit, have a set of protocols you better follow. Ignore them, and you'll be in math quicksand before you know it.

Tip #1: Taming The Beasts
Base and Exponent Relations

When you have the same base and you're multiplying them, add the exponents. For example,

$$2^{2+3} = 2^5$$

Tip #2: Power to the Power
Exponential Inception

Ever see something like (22)3? You just multiply the exponents

$$2^{2*3} = 2^6$$

John's Field Ops: Exponential Wisdom

- **Break It Down:** When faced with a complicated exponent expression, don't hesitate to break it down into simpler forms. It's like disassembling and cleaning your rifle; understand each part before putting it all together.

- **Train Your Mental Muscles:** You know how we run drills to build muscle memory? Same goes for exponents. The more you practice, the quicker you'll be at spotting patterns and solving problems.

- **Dive Deep into Real World Uses:** Did you know that exponents are crucial for things like compound interest and scientific notations? The quicker you master them, the quicker you can apply them to real-world problems—both in and out of uniform.

PRACTICAL ARITHMETIC

Hey, team! So, you're back for more, eh? That's the spirit! Today we're gonna dig deep into the foundational training of the math world—Practical Arithmetic. Yup, you heard me right. This isn't abstract, pie-in-the-sky stuff; it's the basic training of numbers, and it's as real as the mud on your boots.

When I say this is the stuff you use every day, I'm not yanking your chain. Calculating distances for artillery fire, rationing out supplies, or figuring out how many seconds it takes to disarm a bomb—all of it comes down to basic arithmetic. So let's dig in, shall we?

The Big Four: The Infantry of Math

The four operations—addition, subtraction, multiplication, and division—are your go-to grunts. They do the heavy lifting and serve as the backbone for every math operation you'll ever encounter.

Tip #1: Quick-Draw Addition and Subtraction

Time is of the essence. Whether you're counting ammo or calculating your next move, you should be able to add and subtract in your head as naturally as you breathe. The faster you get at this, the better. Drill, baby, drill!

Tip #2: Multiplication as Your Power Play

There are shortcuts in multiplication that can save you time. Master the squares and the multiples of key numbers like 5, 10, and 25. The quicker you can multiply, the more effective you'll be.

Tip #3: Division—Your Tactical Retreat

Sometimes, you have to divide to conquer. When rationing supplies or distributing forces, division comes into play. Know your division tables, but also understand how to estimate. Sometimes "good enough" is all you need to make an informed decision.

The Field Guide to Arithmetic

- **The Rule of Nines:** If you're not sure about your addition or subtraction, use the Rule of Nines to double-check your answer. Add the digits of your numbers. If they reduce to the same single digit, chances are your answer is correct.

- **Estimation is Your Recon:** Sometimes, you just need a ballpark figure. Learn how to round numbers for quick calculations. This is like recon—getting just enough info to make a smart move without wasting time.

- **Train for Real-world Scenarios:** Don't just practice abstract numbers. Apply arithmetic to real tasks—like budgeting, measuring distances, or calculating time. Make it relevant to get the most out of your training.

- **Mental Math is Your Sidearm:** You won't always have a calculator in the field. Practice doing math mentally to keep your skills sharp. It's like the sidearm you carry: not your first choice but invaluable when you need it.

Ratio Routes
Navigating Proportions and Rates

Hey there, navigators! Welcome aboard. Grab your compass and sextant because today we're plotting a course through the mystical waters of Ratios, Proportions, and Rates. Trust me, this stuff's more practical than a Swiss Army knife on a desert island. From fuel ratios to speed and navigation, understanding this will make you a more competent soldier and a smarter civilian. So sit tight, adjust your bearings, and let's get started. Shall we?

Ratios: The Basic Coordinates

A ratio is simply a way to compare two or more things. It's like comparing the number of enlisted soldiers to officers. For example, if there are 10 enlisted soldiers for every officer, the ratio is 10:1.

Tip #1: Simplify, Soldier!
Always break down your ratios to the simplest form. A 20:2 ratio is the same as 10:1. It just looks messier, like a bunk that hasn't been made.

Tip #2: Ratios are Versatile Operatives
You can express ratios as fractions, decimals, or percentages. That's like saying the same thing in English, Morse code, and smoke signals. Adapt the ratio to what suits your situation best.

Proportions: Your Maps and Scales
Ever used a map? Of course you have! Proportions are the same thing but for numbers. It's about scaling up or down while keeping things in proportion.

Tip #1: Cross-Multiplication, Your Tactical Friend
When you have a proportion (like $a/b=c/d$), cross-multiplication is your go-to method for solving proportions, reliable like a sturdy pair of boots.

Tip #2: Percentages Are Just Fancy Proportions
Thinking of percentages as proportions can simplify your life. 50% is just another way to say 1/2 or a ratio of 1:2. Make the connection, and it's like translating a foreign language you already know.

Rates: Your Speed and Velocity
Rates are like ratios but with an extra twist: time. Miles per hour, heart rate, words per minute—these are all rates.

Tip #1: Unit Rates Keep Things Simple
Always break things down to a 'per one' basis if you can. Instead of dealing with 300 miles in 6 hours, think of it as 50 miles per hour. It's easier to scale, adjust, and manipulate.

Tip #2: Dimensional Analysis, Your Passport
When dealing with complex rates, make sure your units are consistent. This is how you convert miles per hour to feet per second or vice versa. Consistency is key, like a steady hand on the wheel.

Captain's Log of Tips and Tricks

- **Double Check Your Compass:** Always validate your proportions and rates. If you're off, it could be a small mistake with big consequences, like mistaking friendlies for hostiles.

- **Pilot Through Real-world Scenarios:** Apply these concepts to real-world situations like calculating fuel efficiency, rate of fire, or navigation bearings. Make it practical!

- **Never Ignore the Small Details:** A tiny shift in a ratio or rate can result in a massive change. Imagine if you're just one degree off on a long voyage—you'll end up miles away from your target.

Percentage Pursuits
Combining Efforts and Percent Calculations

Hey there, team! Ready to dive into another mission briefing? Excellent, because today we're diving deep into the realm of percentages. Now, don't click away just yet! Understanding percentages is like knowing how to zero your rifle. Get it wrong, and you'll miss your mark every time. Get it right, and you'll be on target like a laser-guided missile. So, pull up a chair, recruit. It's time to crack the code of percentages.

Percentages: Your Field Intel
Percent literally means "per 100." Think of percentages as a way to express fractions and decimals in a standard, easily digestible form.

Tip #1: The Power of 1%
1% is your friend—your buddy—your comrade-in-arms. It's 1/100 of a whole. Learn to find 1% of a number, and you can easily find any other percent by scaling up or down.

Tip #2: Conversion is Your Translator
Keep in mind that percentages, decimals, and fractions are like different languages. And in this interna-

tional mission, you gotta be multilingual. For example, 25% is 0.25 is ¼. Learn to switch between them like a pro.

Combining Percentages: Your Tactical Ops
Sometimes you'll encounter situations where you need to add or subtract percentages.

Tip #1: Stacking Up Percentages
If you're applying multiple percentage increases or decreases, do NOT add the percentages together. A 10% increase followed by a 20% increase is NOT a 30% increase. You have to compound them. This is mission-critical, folks.

Tip #2: Averaging Percentages is a No-Go
If one mission was 60% successful and another was 40% successful, the average isn't necessarily 50%. You have to weigh these percentages based on the scale and scope of each mission (or number, in non-military speak).

John's Strategic Guidance: Tips from the Frontlines

- **Real-world Scenarios, Soldier:** Always put your percentages to work. How much fuel will you save if you drive 10% slower? What's the real cost of that 25% discount at the PX?

- **Round and Approximate:** In a firefight, there's no time for a calculator. Learn to round numbers and estimate. Can't figure out 15% in your head? Break it into 10% + 5%, and go from there.

- **Check Your Six:** After doing any percentage calculation, double-check your work. A mistake can cost you, whether you're in the supermarket or on the battlefield.

Statistical Stages
Patterns, Predictions, and Chance Insights

Hey, you math warriors! Gather 'round; Captain John's back with another top-secret briefing. Today, we're veering off the beaten path and taking a recon mission into the jungle of statistics. That's right, statistics—the same subject that, when mastered, can help you make educated guesses, predict outcomes, and even give you the lowdown on chance itself.

You might be wondering, "Why the heck do I need to know this?" Well, soldier, from understanding the likelihood of mission success to making tactical decisions, stats play a big role. So, let's lock and load!

Patterns: Your Clues to the Enemy's Moves
Statistics often start with recognizing patterns. These can be as simple as calculating the average or as complicated as identifying trends.

Tip #1: The Power of the Average
The mean, median, and mode are your basic statistical tools. These are the Swiss Army knives of statistics. Know them well, and you'll always have a quick way to summarize a set of data.

Tip #2: Trends Are Your Forecast
When you see a pattern or trend in data, that's like getting weather intel before a big operation. Use it wisely to predict future scenarios and prepare accordingly.

Predictions: Your Tactical Foresight
Being able to make educated guesses based on past behavior or data sets is like having a pair of binoculars on a recon mission.

Tip #1: Correlation Doesn't Mean Causation
Just because two things happen together doesn't mean one caused the other. Don't mistake your morning jog for causing the sun to rise, soldier!

Tip #2: Use Your Bayesian Brain
In layman's terms, this means updating your predictions based on new data. Get new intel? Adjust your strategy accordingly, just like updating GPS coordinates while on the move.

Chance Insights: The Roll of the Dice
Life's full of uncertainties, and sometimes you have to play the odds. Understanding probability helps you make smarter bets.

Tip #1: The Law of Large Numbers
The more times you roll that dice, the closer you get to the expected average. This is why casinos always win in the long run—and why you should always bet on consistent performance over flukes.

Tip #2: Don't Fall for the Gambler's Fallacy
Thinking that your luck has to change after a losing streak is a rookie mistake. Each roll of the dice is independent of the last.

Nuggets from the Trenches

- **Never Ignore the Outliers:** Sometimes those anomalies and outliers can give you the most valuable intel. Never ignore them; analyze them.

- **Risk Assessment is Your Shield:** Use statistics to evaluate the risks before taking action. Would you rush into a building without knowing what's inside? Didn't think so.

- **Practice, Practice, Practice:** The more you engage with real-world data, the more intuitive all these statistical tools will become. It's like target practice for your brain.

The Final Salute

Well, there you have it, folks—our grand tour through the world of Arithmetic Reasoning, or as I like to call it, "The Tactical Toolbox of Math." From the basics like fractions and decimals to the trickier terrains of percentages and statistics, we've navigated through it all, locked, loaded, and intellectually lethal.

What We've Achieved

We kicked things off by soaring through Fractional Flights, making fractions and decimals as easy to manage as a Sunday stroll. Then, we ascended exponentially with Exponential Elevations, powering through those protocols like a champ. After that, we navigated the turbulent waters of ratios, proportions, and rates in Ratio Routes, steering the ship with finesse. Percentage Pursuits? Nailed it. And, finally, we delved deep into Statistical Stages, where we learned to read patterns, make predictions, and get insights into the vagaries of chance.

Why This Matters

Think of Arithmetic Reasoning as your mental MRE—packed with essential nutrients for your brain, and a critical part of your ASVAB prep. But it's more than that. It's a life skill, as useful off the battlefield as it is on. Budgeting for your family? Planning a project? Gauging risks? This toolbox has got you covered.

John's Final Words of Wisdom

- **Practice Makes Permanent:** Not just perfect, but permanent. The more you practice, the more these concepts will stick with you for life.

- **Context is King:** Always remember to apply these mathematical principles to real-world scenarios. Math isn't just about numbers; it's about problem-solving.

- **Never Stop Learning:** This is a field that always has more to offer. Don't consider this the end, but rather a solid foundation on which to build further skills and knowledge.

Unit III. WORD KNOWLEDGE (WK)

Soldiers, you've got your marching orders: it's time to tackle the Word Knowledge portion of the ASVAB. Now, before you dismiss this as just a bunch of ABCs, let me clue you in on something important. This section is designed to evaluate your understanding and knowledge of words—both in terms of meaning and application. Yep, it tests how well you can pick synonyms, decipher words in context, and make sense of sentences. Trust me, it's more than just a spelling bee; it's about grasping the nuances of language that can serve you well in any MOS (that's Military Occupational Specialty, for the uninitiated). So, buckle up, warriors. We're about to dive deep into the lexicon battlefield, and I'm here to make sure you come out victorious. Ready to step up your word game? Let's navigate this linguistic landscape together, one word at a time!

VOCABULARY MASTERY

Word Foundations
Prefixes, Suffixes, and Structure Insights

Alright, word warriors, listen up! Captain John's back at the helm, and this time we're diving into the nuts and bolts of words. I'm talking about prefixes, suffixes, and the innards of word structure. Knowing these elements is like having a trusty multi-tool in your back pocket. You can disassemble words you've never even seen before, figure out what they mean, and reassemble them to suit your needs. Pure linguistic magic!

Prefixes: The Frontline Foot Soldiers
Think of prefixes as the scouts leading the charge. They're at the front of a word, setting the tone for what's to follow.

Tip #1: Prefixes Set the Mission Objective
When you see 'un-' at the start, you know it's gonna negate the word that follows, like 'unhappy' or 'unarmed.' Knowing this helps you instantly get the gist.

Tip #2: Familiarize Yourself with Common Prefixes
"Re-", "un-", "dis-", "pre-", "mis-"—these are your allies. Get to know them, and you're one step closer to being a word general.

Suffixes: The Snipers in the Back
Suffixes come at the end, and they're your specialized troops. They change the role a word plays in a sentence.

Tip #1: Suffixes Shift the Strategy
Take a verb like 'run' and add "-er," and boom, you've got a noun: 'runner.' That's like going from offense to defense in a heartbeat.

Tip #2: Suffixes are Your Swiss Army Knife
They can turn verbs into nouns, nouns into adjectives, and so on. Learn the common ones like "-ing," "-ly," "-able," and you'll unlock new layers of language.

Structure Insights: The Tactical Blueprint
Every word has an architecture, a sort of backbone that gives it meaning.

Tip #1: Break it Down to Build it Up
When faced with a big, intimidating word, break it into chunks. Identify the prefix, the root, and the suffix. Now you're the engineer, reverse-engineering the word to understand it.

Tip #2: When in Doubt, Refer to Latin or Greek
A lot of English words have Latin or Greek roots. A little etymological background can make you the Sherlock Holmes of vocabulary.

Lessons from the Lexicon

- **Memorization Isn't Enough:** This isn't just about rote learning, folks. It's about understanding the mechanics of words so you can adapt and improvise in any situation.

- **Keep a Word Diary:** Every time you come across a new word, jot it down. Dissect it. Understand it. Make it a part of your vocabulary arsenal.

- **Practice in Context:** Words aren't just isolated units. They work together in sentences, like a well-coordinated squad. So practice using your new vocab in real-world contexts.

Lexicon Layers
Expanding Vocabulary & Tracing Roots

Hey there, language tacticians! Captain John back on the comm, and we've got an important mission today: digging deep into the soil of vocabulary and tracing those roots. You know, the English language is like a dense forest—interconnected, full of hidden trails, and rich with diversity. Understanding the roots of words can be like having a topographical map of that forest. You'll know where you're going and how to get there. So let's roll up our sleeves and start digging, shall we?

Expanding Vocabulary: The Ultimate Arsenal
Look, you can't win battles with just one type of weapon, right? The more weapons you have, the better you'll fare. Similarly, the more words you know, the better you'll express yourself.

Tip #1: Consume Wisely
Read broadly—newspapers, journals, fiction, non-fiction. Every new genre is like a different training ground for vocabulary expansion.

Tip #2: Don't Just Parrot, Understand
When you come across a new word, don't just repeat it. Investigate it. Think of its synonyms, antonyms, and use it in a sentence. Make that word your own.

Tracing Roots: The Ancestral Lineage of Words
You know how every family has a history? Well, words have families too. Understanding a word's root can often reveal its cousins, siblings, and long-lost relatives.

Tip #1: Identify the Family Name
Take a word like 'biology.' The root 'bio-' means life. Now you can easily understand 'biography,' 'biosphere,' or 'biodegradable.' You just met the whole family!

Tip #2: Language Family Reunions are Helpful
Roots often come from Latin, Greek, or other languages. Knowing even a few basic roots from these languages can make you the family historian of English vocabulary.

John's QuickDraw Tips: Fast-Tracking Your Lexicon Skills

- **Flashcards 2.0:** This time, include not just the word and its meaning but also its root, prefix, or suffix. It's like giving your flashcards a performance boost.

- **The Thesaurus is Your Sparring Partner:** Use it regularly. But remember, spar wisely. Know the nuances between similar words.

- **Word of the Day:** Make it a ritual. Learn a new word each day, but also trace its root. That way, you're learning a whole family of words, not just one.

So, there you have it, folks! We've navigated the fascinating layers of the lexicon, equipped with the tools to dig deep, and expand wide. Your mission, should you choose to accept it, is to apply these strategies and make your vocabulary invincible. What's your action plan? Got a word or a root that blew your mind? Share your thoughts, and let's make this a community intelligence operation!

Roots & Routes
Hands-on Exploration and Mastery

Ahoy there, future word warriors! Captain John back in the cockpit and ready to guide you through another exhilarating mission: a deep dive into the roots and routes of words. This is the real-deal tactical training you've been waiting for, where we get our hands dirty and dig up some language gold. No more dabbling on the surface; we're going subterranean! Ready for some spelunking? Buckle up, buttercup, we're goin' in!

Hands-On Exploration: Gettin' Down & Dirty with Roots
So, you've been introduced to word roots, but have you ever rolled up your sleeves and dug into the soil yourself? Time to become a word archaeologist!

Tip #1: The Word Excavation Game
Grab a complex word you've recently encountered—let's say 'misconception.' Now break it down: 'mis-' (wrongly), 'con-' (with), 'cept' (take), '-ion' (the act of). You've just dissected a word like a pro!

Tip #2: The Root Detective
Identify a root and then go on a hunt for words that share that root. It's like a scavenger hunt, but you're bagging words, not treasure—though arguably, they're the same thing.

Routes to Mastery: Navigating the Language Highway
Once you know a word root, you'll start seeing it everywhere. That root can branch off into different directions, creating new words and meanings. The possibilities? Endless!

Tip #1: The Synonym Swap Drill
Take a word you know well. Now use your newly acquired root knowledge to find a fancier version of the same word. It's like swapping a jeep for a tank!

Tip #2: The Root Map
Start with a single root and jot down all the words that stem from it. You'll end up with a roadmap that can take you from 'cycle' to 'encyclopedia' just because you know the root 'cyclo' means 'circle' or 'wheel.'

John's Action-Oriented Intel: Let's Get Moving!

- **Root Journal:** Keep a diary of the roots you discover. Make it your secret playbook.

- **Daily Challenge:** Force yourself to use a new root-based word in a sentence each day. Text it, say it, tweet it—just use it!

- **Talk the Talk:** Use your newfound vocabulary in daily conversations. Yeah, you might get some raised eyebrows at first, but hey, that's how legends are born, my friend.

By the end of this hands-on expedition, you won't just be navigating through language; you'll be blazing new trails. So, how are you planning to become a root-master? Found a fun way to practice? Spill the beans, compadres!

Meaning Mechanics
Decoding & Daily Life Inferences

Heya, verbal virtuosos! Captain John clocking in for another enlightening jaunt into the wild terrain of linguistics. Today's objective? To decode the mechanics of word meanings and see how they fit into the grand scheme of daily life. Let me break it down for you—this is where the rubber meets the road. We're moving beyond just knowing words and roots; we're talking about turning them into daily-life secret weapons. So lace up those boots and affix your bayonets, we're going in!

Decoding: The Nitty-Gritty of Word Anatomy
Decoding isn't just about understanding what a word means. It's about dissecting it, understanding its moving parts, and recognizing the nuances.

Tip #1: The Meaning Safari
Here's a fun game: Pick a word, any word—let's say, 'obstinate.' Now, decode it. 'Ob-' (against), '-stin-' (stand), '-ate' (inclined to). Put it together, and you've got 'inclined to stand against.' Voila! You're a decoding genius.

Tip #2: Context Clues: The Silent Allies

Never forget the value of a word's surrounding environment. Often, the sentence around a tricky word will give you all the intel you need to decode it.

Daily Life Inferences: Your Everyday Tactical Guide

Knowing a word's meaning is one thing; knowing when and how to use it—or understand it—is a whole different battle.

Tip #1: The Eavesdropping Game

Next time you're on public transit or in a cafe, tune into conversations around you. Try to infer the meaning of words you don't know based solely on the context. You'll be surprised how much you can glean.

Tip #2: The Situation Simulation

Think of different scenarios—like a job interview, a date, or even a survival situation. What words might come in handy? List them, decode them, and master them.

John's Tactical Toolbox: Your Go-to Strategies

- **Word Synthesis:** Practice combining different roots, prefixes, and suffixes to form new words. What do they mean? Can you use them in a sentence?

- **Life Linking:** For every new word or root you learn, link it to a real-life object or situation. It'll stick in your memory like glue on paper.

- **Infer & Share:** Whenever you successfully infer a word meaning in real life, jot it down and share it with someone. You'll be reinforcing your own learning and possibly teaching someone else in the process.

Comprehension Cornerstones
Context and Logical Analysis

All right, language commandos! Captain John here again, and you better believe we've got a special recon mission today. We're diving deep into the waters of comprehension, armed with two steadfast cornerstones: Context and Logical Analysis.

These are your flare guns and first aid kits in the wilderness of text and conversation. So, what say we unpack our gear and get down to brass tacks, eh?

Context: The Invisible Guideposts

When it comes to comprehension, context isn't just your friend; it's your guardian angel. It can rescue you from misunderstandings and help you navigate through complex situations.

Tip #1: Be A Context Chameleon

Adapt to your environment. Reading a medical paper? Your understanding of words like "benign" or "malignant" should differ from when you're reading a spy novel. Context sets the stage; don't ignore it.

Tip #2: The Contextual Cross-reference

Sometimes one part of a text can shed light on another. Found a tricky sentence? Look for clues in other parts of the text. It's like asking for directions without actually asking!

Logical Analysis: The Tactical Compass

This cornerstone is about making connections and drawing conclusions. AKA, this is your brain flexing its muscles.

Tip #1: The Syllogism Gym

Remember the classic "All men are mortal; Socrates is a man; therefore, Socrates is mortal"? That's a syllogism. Practice these logical steps to sharpen your analytical skills.

Tip #2: The "What-If" War Games

Challenge yourself with hypothetical scenarios. What if this character had done X instead of Y? How would the story change? This kind of analysis not only deepens your comprehension but also makes for great party conversation.

John's Field Manual Quickies:
Quick & Dirty Tricks to Up Your Game

- **Context Clusters:** Make it a habit to underline or note down words and phrases around difficult terms. These are your contextual breadcrumbs.

- **Logical Journal:** Keep a diary where you jot down your daily decision-making processes. Yep, even choosing between pizza and tacos deserves logical scrutiny.

- **Read Aloud:** Sometimes, hearing the words can make the context and logical connections snap into place. Try it, especially with complex material.

There we have it, troopers! The cornerstones of comprehension are set, and you're now equipped to venture into the complex landscapes of text and conversation. How do you plan to use these tools? Got any success stories or hurdles you've encountered? Let's keep this dialogue going.

Semantic Signals
Navigating Word Tones

Welcome back, linguistic trailblazers! Captain John on the comms, and let me tell you, we're about to tackle a subject that's as tricky as diffusing a time bomb: Semantic Signals. Think of this as understanding the emotional and contextual "color" words carry. It's not just about what words mean; it's about how they feel. Ever say something harmless and have it blow up in your face? Well, it might be because you missed the semantic signals. So grab your compass and flashlight, friends—we're going on a treasure hunt for tone!

Understanding the Signals: Emotional Radar 101
When we communicate, words often carry emotional or contextual baggage. Let's make sure we're tuned into the right frequency.

Tip #1: The Tone Analyzer
Next time you read an article, try to identify its tone. Is it celebratory, critical, or maybe even sarcastic? This will tell you a lot about the writer's intention, which is a key part of understanding the message.

Tip #2: Word Association Gym
Here's a fun exercise: Write down a word and then jot down the first five emotional or contextual associations that come to mind. For example, "Freedom" might conjure "liberty," "USA," "independence," "democracy," and "Fourth of July."

Navigating through Tonal Traffic: The Semantic Street
Sometimes, the tone of a single word can change based on where it's used. We're learning how to read these signals like a pro.

Tip #1: Stoplight Strategy
Think of words as having a 'stoplight' color: red for negative, yellow for neutral, and green for positive. This simple trick can help you quickly assess the tone of a sentence or conversation.

Tip #2: The Detour Maneuver
If you find yourself in a tricky conversation, try to shift the tone by consciously choosing words with different semantic signals. It's like making a tactical detour in a battlefield.

John's Pro-Tips for Signal Mastery: Don't Miss the Signs!

- **Tone Logging:** Keep a diary of interesting sentences you come across, and annotate them for tone. Think of this as your "tone vocabulary."

- **Soundtrack Your Words:** Read sentences aloud and try to inject them with the tone you think they carry. You'll be amazed at how different words can sound based on their intended tone.

- **Ask for Feedback:** If you're not sure about the tone of something you're writing or saying, ask someone for a quick read. Sometimes, a second set of eyes—or ears—can be a real lifesaver.

So, folks, now you're not just word-smart; you're tone-smart. You're geared to navigate through the emotional and contextual jungles of language like never before. How are you planning to put these new skills to the test? Got any tales from the semantic frontlines? I'm all ears!

The Final Salute
Hey word warriors, you've tackled the toughest linguistic challenges head-on! From prefixes to suffixes, and breaking down complex words, you've turned vocabulary into your secret weapon. Remember, this isn't just

about passing a test—it's about mastering communication for your military journey. Keep driving on and stay sharp!

What We've Achieved

All right, you linguistic warriors, we've reached the end of this high-octane tour through Word Knowledge. What a ride, huh? We've trekked through the jungles of prefixes and suffixes, scaled the peaks of vocabulary expansion, decoded the mysteries of meaning, and even ventured into the emotional labyrinth of semantic signals. Whew! You've collected more tools for your verbal toolbox than most people gather in a lifetime.

But let's not kid ourselves; owning a toolbox isn't the goal. The goal is to use it—efficiently and effectively. When you understand words—truly get them—you're not just boosting your ASVAB scores. No, my friends, you're unlocking doors to richer conversations, deeper relationships, and, let me be frank, a fuller life.

Why This Matters

Mastering word knowledge isn't just about acing the ASVAB; it's about enhancing your ability to communicate effectively in all aspects of military life. Whether you're decoding technical manuals, writing reports, or giving clear instructions, a strong vocabulary is essential. These skills will empower you to navigate complex scenarios, understand your peers and superiors, and make informed decisions swiftly and accurately. Strong word knowledge is your foundation for becoming a strategic, effective leader.

John's Final Words of Wisdom

- **Consistency Is Key:** Regularly set aside time to enrich your vocabulary and engage with language. Keep a notebook, use flashcards, play word games. Make it a lifestyle.

- **Share the Wealth:** Don't keep your newfound knowledge to yourself. Engage others in conversations, debate topics, and most importantly, teach someone else. Remember, knowledge isn't just power; it's a gift that keeps on giving.

- **Never Stop Learning:** Word knowledge isn't a 'one and done' deal. Language evolves, and so should you. Keep updating your skills, and don't shy away from unfamiliar terrain.

That's a wrap, team. Whether you're aiming for the stars with your ASVAB scores or just want to wield words like a pro, remember: Your journey doesn't end here. It's a lifelong odyssey, and every day offers a new opportunity to expand your horizons. So, keep those boots laced and your minds open.

Unit IV. PARAGRAPH COMPREHENSION (PC)

First and foremost, a heartfelt salute to you for considering this journey. As we delve into the Paragraph Comprehension section of this guide, let me share a tidbit from my own journey. Back when I was prepping for my ASVAB, I realized that it's not just about number crunching or knowing technical details. It's also about understanding, interpreting, and making sense of the written word. That's where the Paragraph Comprehension section comes into play. So, what's this section all about? Think of Paragraph Comprehension as your personal recon mission into the world of texts. You'll be presented with short passages, followed by questions that test your ability to grasp the main idea, find details, and make logical inferences. Just as in the field, where clear comprehension can be the difference between mission success and failure, this section evaluates how well you can extract pertinent information from written material. I remember a time during a mission when understanding the subtle nuances in a briefing made all the difference. Similarly, mastering this section can give you a significant edge. And the skills you sharpen here? They're not just for the test; they're life skills that will aid you in every briefing, every manual, and every piece of correspondence in your military career. Remember, every operation, no matter how complex, starts with a clear understanding. And that's exactly what the Paragraph Comprehension section is gearing you up for. So, tighten those bootstraps, keep that chin up, and let's dive into the world of texts together!

PARAGRAPH PROFICIENCY

Comprehension Core
Reading Essentials and Fundamentals

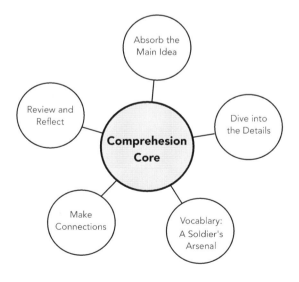

Figure 4.1: A schematic overview of the comprehension process

Think back to a time when you tried to assemble something – maybe a piece of furniture or a gadget. Imagine doing that without any instructions. Daunting, right? That's how crucial understanding written texts is, especially in a military environment where every directive and every mission brief carry weight. Now, onto the essence of comprehension... (Figure 4.1)

- Every text, no matter how intricate, carries a central message or a main idea. Picture it as the backbone of the text. Your first mission? Identify this backbone. Ask yourself: "What's the writer really trying to convey here?"

- Once you've got the main idea down, it's time to focus on the specifics. Details peppered throughout the text add substance to the main idea. Think of these as the essential gear in your toolkit – without them, the task remains incomplete.

- This is where your detective hat comes in. Sometimes, texts won't lay everything out clearly. You'll need to infer or make educated guesses based on the given information. It's like being in the field and connecting the dots to see the bigger picture.

- Words are tools. The more you know, the better equipped you are. If you stumble upon an unfamiliar term, don't retreat. Instead, try to understand its meaning from the surrounding context or look it up. Familiarity with a broad vocabulary is akin to having a well-stocked arsenal – always be prepared!

- After marching through a passage, take a moment to reflect. Summarize what you've read in your own words. This not only reinforces understanding but ensures you've truly grasped the essence of the text.

In our line of work, understanding a piece of intel or a directive can tilt the scales. Mastering reading comprehension isn't just about acing a test; it's about ensuring you're equipped to handle the myriad of situations thrown your way with clarity and precision.

Remember, just as in any mission, the key to conquering comprehension lies in preparation, persistence, and practice. Equip yourself with these fundamentals, and you'll not only decipher texts but truly understand them.

Textual Terrain
Navigating Different Literary Landscapes

Imagine for a moment, navigating through varying terrains – from vast deserts to dense forests, from jagged mountains to serene coastlines. Each terrain demands a different set of skills, equipment, and understanding. Similarly, the world of literature presents a myriad of textual landscapes, each with its own unique features, challenges, and rewards.

Important Textual Landscapes	
Fictional Frontiers	Diving into the world of fiction is akin to exploring vast, unknown lands. While the characters and settings may be products of imagination, the emotions and dilemmas are real. Your mission? Immerse yourself, understand the plot, and connect with the characters. Relate to their emotions, understand their motives, and you'll navigate this terrain like a pro.
Non-Fiction Fields	This terrain is grounded in facts, real events, and concrete information. Like a detailed map, non-fiction offers clarity and direction. Here, your focus is on extracting key data points, understanding real-world implications, and critically analyzing presented arguments
Poetic Pathways	Poetry is the rolling hills of our textual terrain – beautiful, layered, and open to interpretation. It's not just about understanding the words, but feeling their rhythm, sensing the emotions, and deciphering the deeper meanings that lie beneath.
Dramatic Dunes	Drama, with its dialogues and stage directions, offers an immersive experience. Here, you're not just a reader but an active participant, visualizing the scenes, understanding character dynamics, and grasping the underlying themes and conflicts.
Technical Trails	Technical writings, such as manuals or academic papers, are like navigating through a dense forest. They're packed with details, and the path might seem complex. Focus on understanding the main objectives, breaking down complex concepts into digestible chunks, and applying the learned knowledge.

Query Quest
Delving into Question Types and Responses

Envision yourself during a recon operation. To extract valuable intel, you need the right questions. Similarly, on the ASVAB and in many facets of life, asking the right questions and understanding their types can be your secret weapon. But not all questions are created equal. Let's dissect the various types you might encounter and how to tackle them head-on.

1. **Direct Detail Digs:**

   These are straightforward queries that seek specifics from the text. Think of them as your compass – they point directly to the answer within the passage. Your mission? Scan and retrieve.

   Example: After reading a paragraph about the Battle of Normandy, a question might be asked, "In which year did the Battle of Normandy take place?" The answer, directly from the text, would be "1944."

2. **Inferential Inquiries:**

   Now, we're delving into more challenging territory. These questions demand you to be a bit of a detective. The answers aren't directly stated but rather implied. Using your analytical skills and the context, you can deduce the right response.

   Example: After reading a passage describing a soldier's hesitant steps, nervous glances, and sweaty palms, a question might ask, "How was the soldier feeling?" Though the passage doesn't say "nervous," you can infer from the cues that he was anxious.

3. **Comparative Quests:**

   Here, you're required to juxtapose two or more elements from the text, be it characters, themes, or events. It's like comparing the strengths of two different platoons. Understand the unique qualities and see how they relate to one another.

   Example: If you read about two leaders - one being vocal and the other leading by quiet example - a question might be, "How do the leadership styles of the two commanders differ?" Here, you're comparing their approaches based on the passage.

4. **Thematic Trails:**

   These questions go beyond the surface, probing deeper into the core themes or overarching messages of the passage. They're a bit like understanding the broader strategy behind a specific operation.

   Example: After reading a story of a recruit overcoming his limits during a rigorous training regime, a question might ask, "What is the central theme of the story?" Your answer might be "Perseverance in the face of challenges."

5. **Analytical Assessments:**

   Ever evaluated the reliability of a source during a mission? Similarly, these questions ask you to critically examine the text. Is the argument valid? Are there any biases? Hone in on your critical thinking skills and question the text's credibility.

   Example: A passage might discuss a new strategy, backed by one individual's opinion. A question might ask, "Is the strategy's efficacy universally agreed upon in the text?" You'd need to note that only one viewpoint was presented, suggesting a potential bias or lack of universal agreement.

Navigating the sea of questions is no small feat. But, equipped with the right strategies, you'll not only understand the essence of each query but respond with precision and confidence. Remember, every question, regardless of its type, is a doorway to deeper comprehension. And with each one you tackle, you're refining your skills for the ASVAB and beyond.

Detail Dive
From Global Perspectives to Specific Treasures

Just as our world is an intricate tapestry of broad landscapes and minute details, texts too offer overarching ideas dotted with specific treasures of information. Let's embark on this voyage from the vast horizons down to the hidden gems.

- **Global Glimpses:** Before diving into the specifics, always ensure you get a broad view of the textual terrain.

- **Thematic Threads:** Every text, subtly or overtly, is stitched together by themes.

- **Character Chronicles:** The individuals populating our textual universe aren't just names; they're personalities with depth and dimensions.

- **Detail Detections:** Often, the devil is in the details. These are the specific treasures, the nuances that add richness to the text.

- **Contextual Clues:** The environment in which a fact or event is presented can offer invaluable insights.

As we navigate the oceans of information, remember that every dive into a text is an opportunity to extract value, be it from a bird's-eye view or the tiniest of details. Our ability to discern, dissect, and derive meaning from these dives is what separates a casual reader from a true scholar.

Example from one of my personal experiences

The Tactical Training of '89:

Back in 1989, during my early days at Fort Bragg, we underwent one of the most challenging tactical training courses of my military career. Under the leadership of Major Benson, a stern yet fair officer, our unit was introduced to the intricacies of nighttime operations. Benson believed in the element of surprise and often emphasized the advantages of moonlit maneuvers over daytime drills.

One evening, as the waxing crescent moon cast faint shadows over the parade ground, we were briefed on Operation Night Falcon. This simulated mission required us to navigate a dense forest, locate a mock enemy base, and retrieve a designated package – all without being detected by the 'enemy' patrols. The environment was fraught with challenges – from navigating the rough terrains in dim light to communicating silently using hand signals. But it was also during this operation that I forged some of my closest bonds with fellow soldiers, especially Private Ramirez, who became my lifelong friend after we shared the responsibility of leading our group to the objective.

Now, let's craft questions that utilize the techniques from our "Detail Dive" (Figure 4.2):

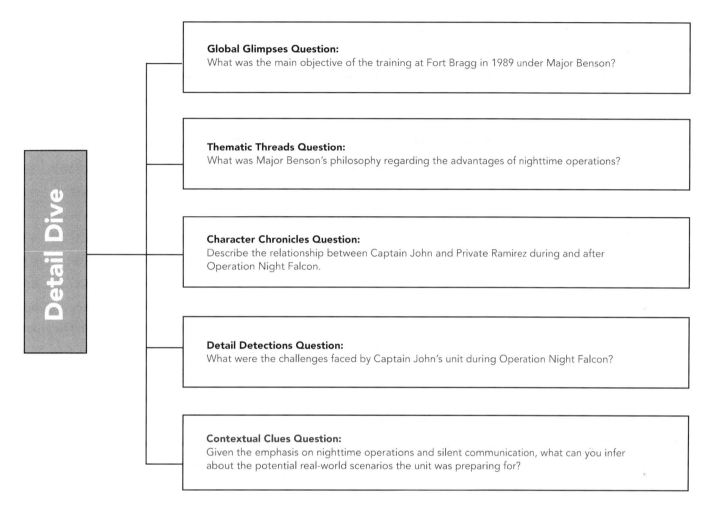

Global Glimpses Question:
What was the main objective of the training at Fort Bragg in 1989 under Major Benson?

Thematic Threads Question:
What was Major Benson's philosophy regarding the advantages of nighttime operations?

Character Chronicles Question:
Describe the relationship between Captain John and Private Ramirez during and after Operation Night Falcon.

Detail Detections Question:
What were the challenges faced by Captain John's unit during Operation Night Falcon?

Contextual Clues Question:
Given the emphasis on nighttime operations and silent communication, what can you infer about the potential real-world scenarios the unit was preparing for?

Figure 4.2: Detail Dive scheme for paragraph comprehension

By answering these questions, one can gain a holistic understanding of the provided paragraph, from broad overviews to the finer nuances.

Inference Intuition
Harnessing Techniques for Deeper Insights

Every text is a landscape, often revealing more in what it doesn't directly state than in what it does. This art of unearthing unspoken truths is what we call 'inference'. While it sounds a touch mysterious, fear not, for with the right approach, you can master it. Here's how we're going to uncover those hidden gems.

1. *Context Clarity:*

   Always take in the broader picture. Understanding the surroundings of a particular statement can provide invaluable clues.

   Example: If you read, "Even with the heavy clouds, Captain Johnson didn't cancel the parade", you can infer that Captain Johnson is likely a strict or highly disciplined leader who wouldn't let weather hinder plans.

2. Emotional Echoes:

Tune into the emotional tone of the text. The sentiments expressed, or even suppressed, can guide your understanding.

> **Example:** Descriptions like "The soldier's hands trembled as he held the letter, his eyes refusing to meet anyone else's" can hint at the soldier's anxiety or fear without explicitly stating it.

3. Word Wisdom:

Sometimes, individual words can carry a weight of implication. Focus on adjectives, adverbs, and any descriptive elements.

> **Example:** In the phrase "The general's curt nod," the word 'curt' suggests that the general might be displeased or impatient.

4. Link and Leap:

Connect various parts of the text to derive conclusions. Combine separate pieces of information to get a fuller picture.

> **Example:** If one sentence mentions how a recruit struggled during training and another highlights his relentless practice sessions, one could infer his determination to overcome challenges.

5. Reflect and Relate:

Think of similar situations or texts you've encountered before. Drawing parallels can be illuminating.

> **Example:** If you've read about the discipline of Spartan soldiers and come across a description of a regiment's strict routines and minimalistic lifestyles, you might infer a Spartan-like ethos.

In the grand dance of comprehension, inference is your flair, your signature move. It's not just about understanding the steps (or words) laid out in front of you, but about adding your unique spin, interpreting the unsaid, and truly making the text come alive. Don't just be content with the surface; dare to dive deeper. Remember, every line of text holds a world of insights, just waiting for an intuitive mind to uncover. Train that mind to be yours.

The Final Salute

Well, cadet, our journey through the maze of paragraph comprehension is coming to a pause, but remember, true mastery is an ongoing expedition. When I was a young lieutenant, fresh out of the academy, I was handed a mission dossier filled with complex intelligence reports. The weight of responsibility was immense. At first glance, I was overwhelmed by the sheer volume of information. But, taking a moment, I recalled the skills of reading, understanding, and inferring I had honed over the years. Slowly, patterns emerged, hidden insights revealed themselves, and I was able to draft a successful mission strategy. That operation, against all odds, was a triumph. Not just for its successful execution, but for reaffirming my belief in the power of comprehension.

What We've Achieved

In this chapter, you've navigated the intricate world of Paragraph Comprehension. You've mastered the art of extracting main ideas, identifying key details, and making logical inferences from various texts. From understanding the core of a message to analyzing different literary landscapes, you've sharpened your ability to interpret and synthesize information. These skills are crucial, not just for the ASVAB, but for every mission and directive you'll encounter in your military career. Your enhanced comprehension abilities will serve as a vital asset in any situation.

Why This Matters

The landscape of text is vast, with valleys of explicit details and peaks of hidden insights. As you traverse this terrain, arm yourself with curiosity, intuition, and persistence. Know that the ability to comprehend isn't just about acing a test, but about navigating the complexities of life and the challenges of any mission you might face in the future.

Stay hungry for knowledge, cadet. With every paragraph you dissect, with every inference you draw, you're not only preparing for the ASVAB but fortifying yourself for life's many battles. And always remember, every expert, every seasoned officer, once stood where you stand now: on the threshold of mastery, ready to leap.

John's Final Words of Wisdom

- **Stay Sharp:** Regularly read diverse materials to keep your comprehension skills honed. Continuous practice ensures you're always ready.

- **Context is Crucial:** Always consider the broader context of any text. It helps you grasp the full meaning and nuances.

- **Be Inquisitive:** Never stop questioning and analyzing what you read. A curious mind is a sharp mind.

- **Embrace Challenges:** Difficult texts are opportunities to improve. Face them head-on and learn from every experience.

So, lace up those boots, hold that head high, and march forward with confidence. The world of text awaits, and you, my friend, are more than ready to conquer it.

Unit V. MATHEMATICS KNOWLEDGE (MK)

As we pivot to the Mathematical Knowledge (MK) section, we're entering a realm that is both ancient and supremely relevant to our modern world. Now, don't be daunted by the memories of your school math classes. The MK section is more than just numbers and formulas; it's about logical thinking, problem-solving, and strategic planning. Essential skills, I might add, that every service member needs, whether you're plotting coordinates for a drop zone or managing supplies for a platoon.

Here some crucial points as we embark on this journey:

- **Foundation First:** We'll begin by building a robust foundation, revisiting essential mathematical concepts. You'd be surprised how much can be achieved with a solid grasp of the basics.

- **Real-world Relevance:** Along the way, I'll share stories and examples from my time in service, showing you the real-world applications of mathematical principles.

- **Practice Makes Perfect:** Just as in physical training, consistency is key. Regular practice is the bridge between understanding a concept and mastering it.

- **Mind Over Math:** Lastly, remember that your mindset is half the battle. Approach each problem with an open mind and a willingness to learn.

Brace yourself for an exhilarating journey through the world of math. With persistence, dedication, and the right strategies, you'll conquer this section and be well-prepared for the challenges that lie ahead.

ALGEBRA ESSENTIALS

Expression Basics
From Math's Foundation to Terms

Think of expressions as the language of mathematics, a universal code that transcends borders and time.

Foundation Stone: What is an Expression?
At its core, a mathematical expression is a combination of numbers, variables, and operators. Just as sentences in English are made up of words, expressions in math are constructed from these basic elements. They convey information without necessarily stating a definitive answer.

Numbers and Variables:
Numbers are constants; their value is fixed. Be it **3**, **-7**, or **2.5**, they remain unchanging. Variables, on the other hand, are the wild cards – represented by letters like x, y, or z. Their values can vary, giving math its flexibility and adaptability.

Operators – The Action Heroes:
Operators tell us what to do with numbers and variables. Addition (**+**), subtraction (**-**), multiplication (*****), and division (**/**) are the primary ones, guiding the interactions between numbers and variables.

Terms and Their Friends:

A term can be a standalone number, a variable, or a combination of both. For example, **7**, x, and **7x** are all terms. When you combine terms with operators, you get a full-blown expression!

Now, here's a little nugget from my time in the service. During a particularly complex logistical mission, I remember using basic algebraic expressions to quickly estimate the supplies we'd need. By assigning variables to uncertain quantities and working through the problem, we managed a successful operation with minimal waste. That's the real-world magic of understanding and applying math's foundational expressions.

Equation Evolution
Single to Twofold Variables

Imagine for a moment that math is a symphony, with each equation playing its unique note. As we progress, the composition becomes more intricate, but oh, the melodies we can create! Our next foray into the mathematical universe will be a step up – moving from single to twofold variables. Ready to conduct this orchestra of numbers?

The Lone Ranger: Single Variable Equations

We begin our journey with equations involving a solitary variable, often represented as x or y. These are the equations where our objective is to find the value of this lone variable. For instance, $3x = 12$. Here, the mystery we need to solve is: what is x?

Double Trouble: Twofold Variable Equations

As we elevate our mathematical prowess, we encounter equations with two variables. Consider $2x + y = 10$. Now, there's an added layer of complexity. Not only are we determining x, but y also enters the picture. Such equations often come in pairs or systems, giving us enough information to find both variables.

Plotting the Path:

With twofold variables, a beautiful aspect emerges: the power to visualize them on a graph. Each equation represents a line, and the point where they meet, if they do, represents their solution.

Real-world Resonance

To give you a slice from my service days, I once had to coordinate two teams for a joint mission. Each team's speed and approach (represented by x and y) had to be synchronized. By treating their routes and speeds as twofold variables, we created a plan where both teams met at the rendezvous point right on time. That, my friend, was math in action on the ground.

Systematic Solutions
Tackling Multiple Equations

In the realm of mathematical knowledge, mastering the skill of solving multiple equations at the same time is essential. These equations can appear daunting at first, but with systematic approaches like substitution, elimination, and matrix methods, they become manageable. This section will guide you through these techniques, ensuring that you're equipped to tackle these challenges effectively.

1. **Substitution Method**

   When using the substitution method, you first solve one of the equations for one variable. Then, you take that solution and plug it into the other equation. This approach works best when one of the equations can be easily solved for one of the variables

   ### Example:
   Consider the equations:

   $$x + y = 10$$

   $$2x - y = 3$$

Solve the first equation for:

$$y = 10 - x$$

Now substitute this into the second equation:

$$2x - (10 - x) = 3$$

Solve for x:

$$2x - 10 + x = 3$$

$$3x = 13$$

Now substitute x back into the first equation to find y :

$$y = 10 - \frac{13}{3} = \frac{17}{3}$$

So,

$$x = \frac{13}{3}, \quad y = \frac{17}{3}$$

2. Elimination Method

In the elimination method, you line up two equations and either add or subtract them to cancel out one of the variables. This technique simplifies the system, making it easier to solve

Example:
Consider the same equations:

$$x + y = 10$$

$$2x - y = 3$$

Align them and add:

$$(x + y) + (2x - y) = 10 + 3$$

$$3x = 13$$

Substitute x into one of the original equations to find y, as shown in the substitution method.

3. Matrix Method

For systems with more variables or more complex equations, the matrix method can be an efficient tool. This involves creating matrices from the co-efficients of the variables and then applying matrix operations to solve the system.

Example:
Consider a system of equations:

$$x + 2y = 5$$

$$3x - y = 6$$

First, write the coefficient matrix and the constant matrix:

$$\begin{bmatrix} 1 & 2 \\ 3 & -1 \end{bmatrix}, \quad \begin{bmatrix} 5 \\ 6 \end{bmatrix}$$

Now, use matrix operations (like row reduction) to solve for x and y. This method is more complex and typically requires a calculator or a deeper understanding of matrix algebra.

Conclusion

Each of these methods has its place depending on the nature of the equations involved. Mastery of these techniques ensures that you are well-equipped to tackle a variety of problems involving multiple equations, a skill that is beneficial not only for the ASVAB but in many real-world applications, particularly in technical and engineering fields. Practice is key to becoming proficient in these methods, so it's advisable to work through various problems to solidify your understanding and efficiency.

Quadratic Quest

Venturing into Variable Equations

Embarking on the journey of understanding quadratic equations is like unlocking a new level in mathematical problem-solving. Quadratics are polynomial equations of the second degree, typically: $ax^2 + bx + c = 0$

They are fundamental in many areas (e.g. engineering, physics, economics) and are crucial for standardized tests like the ASVAB.

A quadratic equation is characterized by its standard form $ax^2 + bx + c = 0$ where a, b and c are constants and $a \neq 0$. The solutions to these equations, known as the roots, can be real or complex and are found using various methods

Methods to Solve Quadratic Equations

Factoring:

This involves expressing the quadratic equation as a product of its factors.

Example:
Consider:
$$x^2 - 5x + 6 = 0$$
Factorize to:
$$(x - 2)(x - 3) = 0$$
The solutions are $x = 2$ and $x = 3$.

Quadratic Formula:
A universal method applicable to all quadratic equations is the quadratic formula:
$$x = \frac{-b \pm \sqrt{b^2 - 4ac}}{2a}$$

Example:
For:
$$2x^2 - 4x - 6 = 0$$

Simplify to find the values of x:
$$x = \frac{-4 \pm \sqrt{(-4)^2 - 4(2)(6)}}{2(2)}$$

Completing the Square:
This method involves rearranging the equation to form a perfect square trinomial.

Example:
$$x^2 + 6x + 9 = 0$$
Rewrite as:
$$(x + 3)^2 = 0$$
Solve for x, giving $x = -3$.

Graphical Interpretation

Quadratic equations graph as parabolas (Figure 5.1). The roots of the equation correspond to the points where the parabola intersects the x-axis. Understanding the graph can provide valuable insights into the nature of the solutions.

- **Vertex:** The highest or lowest point on the parabola. It can be found using the formula.
$$\left(-\frac{b}{2a} \right), f\left(-\frac{b}{2a} \right)$$

- **Axis of Symmetry:** A vertical line that passes through the vertex, dividing the parabola into two symmetrical halves.

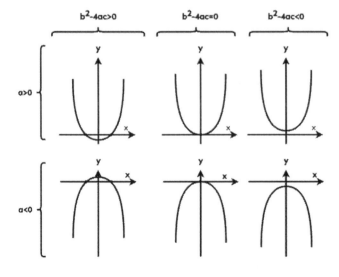

Quadratic Function: y=ax²+bx+c=0

Figure 5.1: Different Graphs for a Quadratic Function

Applications and Conclusion

In real-world scenarios, especially in military contexts, quadratic equations can model trajectories, optimize designs, and solve rate problems, among other applications. Mastery of quadratic equations enhances problem-solving skills, making it a valuable asset for ASVAB preparation and beyond.

Inequality Insights
Setting and Reading Boundaries

Inequalities are fundamental in mathematics, expressing the concept that one value is less than, greater than, or simply not equal to another. Understanding how to set and read these inequalities is vital for problem-solving in various scenarios, including those presented in the ASVAB. Let's dive into the world of inequalities to understand their principles and applications.

Understanding Inequalities

Inequality compares two values, showing if one is greater, less, or unequal to the other. The primary inequality symbols are:

- **Greater Than (>):** Indicates that the value on the left is larger than the value on the right. For example, $x > 5$ means that x is any number greater than 5.

- **Less Than (<):** Implies that the value on the left is smaller than the one on the right. $y < 3$ indicates that y is any number less than 3.

- **Greater Than or Equal To (≥):** Shows that the value on the left is either greater than or equal to the value on the right. $a \geq 7$ means a is 7 or more.

- **Less Than or Equal To (≤):** Indicates the value on the left is either less than or equal to value on the right. b≤4 implies b b is 4 or less.

Solving Inequalities

Similar to equations, inequalities can be solved by adding, subtracting, multiplying, or dividing both sides by the same number. However, a critical rule to remember is that multiplying or dividing by a negative number reverses the inequality sign.

Example:
If you have $-2x > 6$, to solve for x, you divide both sides by -2, remembering to reverse the inequality:

$$-\frac{2x}{-2} < \frac{6}{-2}$$
$$x < -3$$

Graphical Representation
Inequalities can be graphically represented on a number line, where:

A filled dot indicates the number is included in the solution (≥ or ≤).

An open dot means the number is not part of the solution (> or <).

Example:
Graphing x>5 would involve an open dot at 5 and a line extending to the right, indicating all numbers greater than 5.

Applications in Test Scenarios and Beyond
In test scenarios like the ASVAB, understanding inequalities can help in problems involving range, limits, and boundary conditions. In practical military applications, inequalities might be used to establish parameters for safe operational boundaries, load limitations, or strategic planning thresholds.

GEOMETRY FOUNDATIONS

Welcome to the world of Geometry, a fundamental branch of mathematics focused on the characteristics and connections of points, lines, surfaces, solids, and even higher-dimensional analogs. This chapter, "Geometry Foundations," is designed to guide you through the essential concepts and principles of geometry, laying a strong groundwork for understanding spatial relationships, shapes, and their properties. Whether you're preparing for the ASVAB, planning a career in a field that requires spatial awareness, or simply looking to strengthen your mathematical acumen, this journey into geometry will equip you with the tools and insights needed to navigate the world of shapes and spaces with confidence and clarity.

In this section, we'll delve into the basics of geometry, including angles, lines, circles, triangles, and other polygons, exploring how they interact and form the building blocks of our physical world. From the precision required in engineering and architecture to the strategic planning in military operations, a solid grasp of geometric principles is invaluable. Let's embark on this journey of discovery, where every shape tells a story, and every spatial relationship opens a door to a new understanding.

Linear & Angular
Navigating Lines and Their Intersections

The study of lines and angles forms the bedrock of geometric understanding. In this section, "Linear & Angular: Navigating Lines and Their Intersections," we will explore the fundamental concepts of linear and angular geometry. This exploration is not just about understanding shapes and patterns; it's about decoding the language of the universe as expressed through geometry.

Linear Geometry
The Study of Lines

Linear geometry focuses on the properties and relations of lines. Key concepts include:

- **Parallel Lines:** Two lines that never meet, no matter how far they are extended.

- **Perpendicular Lines:** Lines that meet at a right angle (90 degrees).

- **Intersecting Lines:** Lines that meet or cross at any angle.

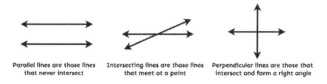

Parallel lines are those lines that never intersect | Intersecting lines are those lines that meet at a point | Perpendicular lines are those that intersect and form a right angle

Figure 5.3: Types of Lines

Angular Geometry
The Realm of Angles

Angles are formed when two lines meet or intersect. Understanding angles is crucial for solving a wide range of geometric problems:

- **Acute Angle:** An angle smaller than 90 degrees.

- **Obtuse Angle:** An angle between 90 degrees and 180 degrees.

- **Right Angle:** An angle measuring precisely 90 degrees, often marked with a small square in diagrams.

- **Straight Angle:** An angle of 180 degrees, appearing as a straight line.

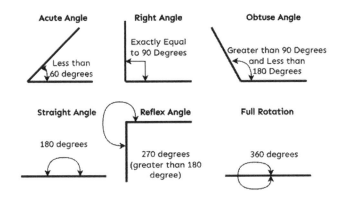

Figure 5.4: Types of Angles

Intersections and Their Implications
The intersection of lines creates angles and shapes, forming the basis of much of geometry:

- **Vertex:** The point where two lines intersect.

- **Angle Measurement:** Using a protractor to measure the size of an angle formed by intersecting lines.

- **Bisectors:** A line or ray that divides an angle or a line segment into two equal parts.

Applications in Real-World Scenarios
Linear and angular geometry play a critical role in various fields:

- **Architecture and Engineering:** Understanding the principles of lines and angles is crucial for designing structures and mechanical systems.

- **Military Strategy:** The use of angular and linear calculations in navigation, targeting, and strategic planning.

ASVAB Focus
For the ASVAB, a firm grasp of linear and angular geometry will aid in solving many of the test's spatial and problem-solving questions. It's essential to understand how lines and angles interact and how to apply this knowledge to both theoretical and practical questions.

Shape Scope
Polygons and Their Dynamics

In the fascinating world of geometry, polygons stand out as some of the most intriguing and essential figures. "Shape Scope: Polygons and Their Dynamics" is a journey into the realm of these multi-sided shapes, exploring their properties, classifications, and the principles that govern their structure. Whether in the pursuit of ASVAB preparation or in the application of practical skills, understanding polygons is indispensable.

Understanding Polygons
A polygon is a closed, two-dimensional shape formed by straight lines. Key aspects include:

- **Vertices:** The points where two sides of a polygon meet.

- **Sides:** The straight-line segments that make up the polygon.

- **Interior Angles:** The angles inside the polygon, at each vertex.

Classifying Polygons
Polygons are classified by the number of sides they possess:

- **Triangles (3 sides):** Including equilateral, isosceles, and scalene triangles.

- **Quadrilaterals (4 sides):** Such as squares, rectangles, and parallelograms.

- **Pentagons (5 sides), Hexagons (6 sides), and so on.**

Each class of polygon has its unique properties and formulas for calculating area and perimeter.

Figure 5.5: Types of Polygons

Regular vs. Irregular Polygons

- **Regular Polygons:** All sides and angles are equal. Examples include a square or an equilateral triangle.

- **Irregular Polygons:** Sides and angles are not all equal. An example would be a scalene triangle.

Polygon Dynamics

Understanding the dynamics of polygons involves:

- **Sum of Interior Angles:** You can find the sum of the interior angles of a polygon using the formula $180(n - 2)$ where n is the number of sides.

- **Exterior Angles:** The exterior angles of a polygon, created by extending one side, always add up to 360 degrees.

Applications in Various Fields

Polygons are prevalent in numerous fields:

- **Architecture and Design:** The use of polygons in planning layouts and designs.

- **Military Applications:** Understanding polygons is crucial in navigation, map reading, and strategic planning.

ASVAB and Beyond

In the ASVAB, questions related to polygons may involve calculating areas, perimeters, or understanding the properties of different shapes. Beyond the exam, polygons are foundational in various technical and practical applications, underscoring their importance in both academic and real-world contexts.

Circular Compass
Circle Properties and Mysteries

In the realm of geometry, the circle is a marvel of symmetry and simplicity. "Circular Compass: Circle Properties and Mysteries" delves into the fascinating attributes of circles, exploring their unique properties

and the mathematical principles they embody. From the ASVAB to practical applications in various fields, a comprehensive understanding of circles is an invaluable asset.

Defining the Circle

A circle is a closed shape with all points at the same distance from its center. This distance is known as the radius. Circles are defined by several key elements:

- **Center:** The fixed point from which the radius extends.

- **Radius (r):** The distance from the center to any point on the circle.

- **Diameter (d):** A straight line passing through the center, connecting two points on the circle's boundary. It is twice the radius.

- **Circumference (C):** The perimeter or boundary line of the circle.

Fundamental Properties of Circles

- **Circumference Formula:** $C = 2\pi r$ or $C = \pi d$, where π *(pi)* is a constant approximately equal to 3.14159 .

- **Area:** The area A of a circle is given by $A = \pi r^2$

Understanding Circle Geometry

- **Chords:** A line segment with both endpoints on the circle. The diameter is a special case of a chord.

- **Arcs:** A segment of the circle's circumference. The length of an arc depends on the central angle that subtends it.

- **Sectors:** A region enclosed by two radii and an arc. Sectors resemble a 'slice of pie' in a circle

Mysteries of the Circle

Circles are rich in mathematical properties and mysteries:

- Pi $(\pi \backslash pi\pi)$: An irrational number representing the ratio of the circumference of a circle to its diameter, approximately equal to 3.14159.

- **Tangents:** A line that touches the circle at exactly one point. The tangent is perpendicular to the radius at the point of contact.

- **Inscribed Angles:** An angle formed by two chords in a circle that meet at a common endpoint. These angles have unique properties related to the arcs they intercept.

Circles in Practical Applications

The properties of circles have practical implications in various fields:

- **Engineering and Design:** Circles are fundamental in designing gears, wheels, and circular structures.

- **Astronomy and Physics:** Circular orbits and trajectories are foundational concepts in these sciences.

- **Art and Architecture:** Circles are used for their aesthetic appeal and structural integrity.

ASVAB Focus

For the ASVAB, understanding the basic properties of circles is essential. Questions may involve calculating the area, the circumference, or understanding the relationships between angles and arcs within a circle.

Dimensional Dive
From 3D Forms to Composite Constructs

As we move beyond the two-dimensional realm into the world of three-dimensional geometry, "Dimensional Dive: From 3D Forms to Composite Constructs" opens up a space where depth, volume, and complexity add layers to our understanding of shapes. This exploration is crucial for a comprehensive grasp of ge-

ometry, especially for those preparing for the ASVAB, and for anyone interested in the practical applications of 3D shapes in various fields like engineering, architecture, and design.

Understanding 3D Shapes

Three-dimensional shapes, or solids, have depth in addition to width and height. Key types include:

- **Prisms:** Solids with two identical polygonal bases and rectangular sides. The volume is found by multiplying the base area by the height.

- **Cylinders:** Shapes with circular bases and a curved surface. The volume formula is $V = \pi r^2 h$ where r is the radius of the base, and h is the height.

- **Pyramids:** Solids with a polygon base and triangular sides that converge at a point (apex). The volume is one-third the product of the base area and the height.

- **Cones:** Similar to pyramids but with a circular base. The volume is $V = \frac{1}{3}\pi r^2 h$

- **Spheres:** Round solids where every point on the surface is equidistant from the center. The volume of a sphere is $V = \frac{4}{3}\pi r^3$

Composite Constructs

Often, real-world objects are made up of a combination of these basic shapes, known as composite solids. Understanding how to break down these objects into simpler shapes and calculate their volume or surface area is a valuable skill.

Applications in Real-World Scenarios

Three-dimensional shapes and constructs are prevalent in numerous fields:

- **Architecture and Construction:** From designing buildings to calculating material quantities, 3D geometry is fundamental.

- **Manufacturing and Design:** Creating and analyzing product designs often require an understanding of three-dimensional shapes.

- **Navigation and Strategy:** In military operations, understanding the terrain and structures involves interpreting three-dimensional spaces.

ASVAB Focus
For the ASVAB, proficiency in handling 3D geometry questions will aid in sections that assess spatial awareness and technical knowledge. You might encounter questions involving volume calculations, surface area estimations, or understanding the structure of composite solids.

Planar Precision
Mastering Coordinate Geometry

In the mathematical landscape, coordinate geometry, also known as analytic geometry, stands as a critical domain where algebra meets geometry. "Planar Precision: Mastering Coordinate Geometry" is designed to guide you through the fundamentals of this subject, emphasizing the importance of precision and analytical skills in interpreting and solving problems on the coordinate plane. This section is especially relevant for those preparing for the ASVAB, as well as for anyone interested in fields that combine spatial understanding with algebraic calculations.

Fundamentals of Coordinate Geometry
Coordinate geometry revolves around the coordinate plane, a two-dimensional grid defined by a horizontal axis (x-axis) and a vertical axis (y-axis). The intersection of these axes forms the origin, typically labeled as point $(0, 0)$.

Key concepts include:

- **Points:** Defined by coordinates (x, y), where 'x' represents the horizontal position, and 'y' represents the vertical position.

- **Lines:** Represented by equations in the format $y = mx + b$, where m is the slope (steepness) and b is the *y-intercept* (point where the line crosses the *y-axis*).

Slopes and Intercepts
Understanding slopes and intercepts is crucial:

- *Slope (m):* Indicates the direction and steepness of a line. Calculated as $m = \frac{\text{rise}}{\text{run}} = \frac{\text{change in } y}{\text{change in } x}$

- *Y-intercept (b):* The point where the line intersects the *y-axis*.

Equations of Lines
Different forms of line equations are used in coordinate geometry:

- **Slope Intercept Form:** $y = mx + b$, ideal for graphing or when the slope and *y-intercept* are known.

- **Point-Slope Form:** $y - y_1 = m(x - x_1)$, useful when the slope and a specific point on the line are given.

- **Standard Form:** $Ax + By = C$, where A, B, and C are integers.

Analyzing Graphs
Coordinate geometry also involves interpreting and creating graphs:

- **Plotting Points:** Determining the location of points based on their coordinates.

- **Graphing Lines:** Drawing lines based on their equations.

- **Identifying Shapes:** Recognizing geometric shapes and their properties on the coordinate plane.

Applications in Practical Scenarios

Coordinate geometry is used extensively in fields like engineering, architecture, and navigation. In the military, it's crucial for tasks like mapping, targeting, and strategic planning.

ASVAB Focus

In the ASVAB, coordinate geometry questions may involve interpreting graphs, finding slopes, or calculating intercepts. A solid grasp of these concepts will aid in solving these problems efficiently.

The Final Salute

As we bring this chapter on Mathematics Knowledge to a close, it's important to reflect on the journey we've embarked upon. From the fundamental operations of arithmetic to the complexities of coordinate geometry, each section has been a step in building a robust mathematical foundation. This journey is more than just preparation for the ASVAB; it's an exploration of the language of logic, patterns, and problem-solving that underpins so much of the world around us.

What We've Achieved

We navigated through a range of topics:

- **Arithmetic Mastery:** Where numbers are the basic building blocks of more complex operations.

- **Algebraic Concepts:** Unlocking the power of unknowns and variables.

- **Geometry Foundations:** Where shapes and spatial understanding came to life.

- **Advanced Topics:** Including quadratic equations, coordinate geometry, and three-dimensional forms, each adding depth and dimension to our mathematical understanding.

Why This Matters

The skills and concepts covered in this chapter are not confined to the pages of textbooks or the boundaries of classrooms. They extend into everyday life, critical thinking, and various careers, especially in the military, where precise calculations, strategic planning, and problem-solving are integral to success. In the military, mathematics is an essential tool. Whether it's in navigation, logistics, engineering, or cryptography, the principles of mathematics play a crucial role in operational effectiveness and strategic decision-making.

As you move forward, whether towards taking the ASVAB or applying these skills in real-life situations, remember that mathematics is a dynamic and powerful tool. It's a language that, once understood, opens up endless possibilities for analysis, innovation, and problem-solving.

John's Final Words of Wisdom

- **Embrace the challenges:** The effort you put in now lays the groundwork for future successes, both on the ASVAB and in your prospective military career.

- **Carry forward:** the precision, logic, and analytical skills you've honed here, for they are not just answers to test questions, but keys to unlocking challenges you'll encounter in the future.

So, as you close this chapter, take a moment to appreciate the journey you've made and look forward to the paths that your newfound mathematical knowledge will illuminate.

Unit VI. ELECTRONICS INFORMATION (EI)

Aspiring servicemembers! In my 25 years of service and teaching, I've witnessed the indispensable role that a solid understanding of electronics plays, from everyday tasks to mission-critical scenarios. We'll begin by delving into the foundational elements of electricity, exploring currents and resistance—trust me, mastering these basics was a lifesaver during impromptu field radio repairs. Next, we'll navigate through the diverse world of circuits, understanding that a well-constructed circuit can be as crucial as a well-executed mission strategy. Venturing further, we'll uncover the secrets of semiconductors, diodes, and transistors, components that proved essential during specialized reconnaissance missions. The evolution from batteries to Alternating Current (AC) mirrors the adaptive nature of battlefield tactics, emphasizing the importance of versatile energy utilization. Decoding Ohm's Law and digital circuitry principles are next on our agenda, fundamentals that were my go-to when troubleshooting equipment in the field. Communication, the backbone of any operation, will have us delving into the chronicles of radio waves and wireless technology, reflecting on instances when secure communication was the linchpin of mission success. A toolbox tour will introduce you to multimeters, oscilloscopes, and crucial safety protocols, arming you with the knowledge to navigate any electronic challenge. Finally, drawing on years of experience and lessons learned, I'll share valuable insights and strategies to help you triumph in the EI Section, not just as a test but as a stepping stone to a successful military career. So, let's gear up and unlock the doors to electronic mastery together!

ELECTRONIC ESSENTIALS

Electricity Unearthed
From Current to Resistance

Imagine electricity as the lifeblood of all electronic devices, much like the coordination and communication that keep a unit functioning seamlessly.

Current: The Flowing Charge
Current is the heartbeat of electricity, representing the flow of electric charge. It's akin to soldiers moving in unison, each carrying energy from one point to another. The unit of current is the Ampere (A). Think of it as the number of soldiers (electrons) marching past a point per second.

Voltage: The Electric Force
Voltage is the electric force that propels the current forward, much like the orders from a commanding officer motivating the troops. Measured in Volts (V), it's the difference in electric potential energy between two points in a circuit. Higher voltage means a stronger force pushing the current.

Resistance: The Opposition
Every mission encounters obstacles, and in the world of electricity, this obstacle is resistance. Resistance slows down the current, acting like challenging terrain for the marching soldiers. It's measured in Ohms (Ω), and materials with higher resistance make it harder for current to flow, just like rough terrains make marching a tedious task to accomplish.

Circuitry Compass
Series, Parallel, and Beyond

Having unearthed the basics of electricity, let's set our compass towards understanding the different types of circuitry - namely series, parallel, and beyond! This knowledge is the compass that has guided me through countless missions, ensuring our equipment was always in top shape (Figure 6.1).

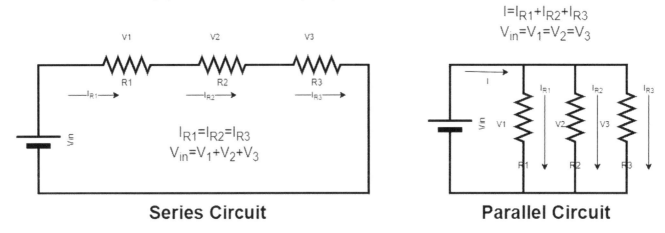

Figure 6.1: Currents and Voltages in Series and Parallel Circuits

First off, Series Circuits are like a one-way street. All components are connected end-to-end in a single path, so the current flows through every component. However, if one component fails, the whole circuit goes down – I've seen this happen, and let me tell you, it's crucial to quickly identify and rectify any issue to maintain functionality.

Next up, Parallel Circuits – these are your multi-lane highways. Components are arranged with their heads connected together, and tails connected. Each component has its own separate path for the current. The beauty here is if one path fails, the others remain unaffected. This redundancy has been a lifesaver in critical situations out in the field.

But we won't stop there – we're going beyond! There are also Complex Circuits, combinations of series and parallel, creating a roadmap of multiple paths with different components. Understanding and navigating these is like planning a meticulous military strategy – every component, every path has its role and impact on the overall operation.

These varied circuit types are the backbone of the electronic devices you'll encounter. I've used this knowledge countless times – whether improvising a device in the field or troubleshooting communication equipment. So, equip yourself with this circuitry compass – it'll guide you through the intricate landscape of electronics, enabling you to face any challenge with confidence and skill.

Semiconductor Saga
Diodes, Transistors, and Their Secrets

I can tell you, understanding the secrets of diodes and transistors has been akin to decrypting enemy codes, unlocking a world of possibilities in the electronic landscapes of our operations.

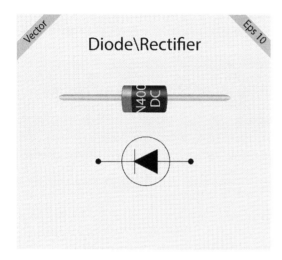

Figure 6.2: Diode is used for uni-directional current flow

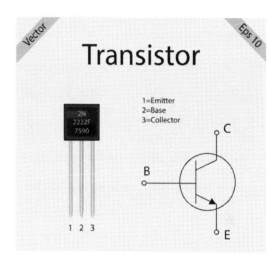

Figure 6.3: Transistor is used for switching applications

Firstly, let's talk about diodes (Figure 6.2). These little components allow current to flow in one direction only – think of them as the gatekeepers, letting the good guys in and keeping the unwanted out. I've used diodes during my service to protect our equipment from electrical malfunctions, ensuring smooth operations when the pressure was on.

Next, we venture into the world of transistors (Figure 6.3). These are the true heroes in the electronic battlefield, acting as switches and amplifiers. They can turn a signal on or off and amplify it, making them indispensable in devices like radios and amplifiers. I recall times in covert operations where the proper functioning of transistors in our communication gear made the difference between mission success and failure.

Understanding the role and functionality of diodes and transistors is fundamental. They are the building blocks of the electronic devices you'll encounter in your service. Mastering their secrets is like learning a new tactical language, enabling you to communicate effectively and adapt swiftly in the dynamic electronic environments you'll navigate.

These semiconductors have their secrets, but once unlocked, they empower you to create, innovate, and troubleshoot on the fly, a skill set that has proven invaluable in my years of service. So let's embrace the semiconductor saga, uncover their secrets, and build a strong foundation for our electronic endeavors!

Energy Evolution
Batteries to Alternating Current (AC)

Future servicemembers! Strap in, as we're about to explore the dynamic evolution of energy, from the humble battery to the ubiquitous Alternating Current (AC). These forms of energy are the lifeblood of our equipment, and understanding them has been crucial during my deployments, keeping our gear operational and our missions on track.

Lead Acid   Lithium   Saltwater

Figure 6.4: A Battery Provides Direct Current Only

Figure 6.5: A Generator can produce Alternating Current used in our homes

We kick off with batteries, the portable powerhouses. They store chemical energy and convert it into electrical energy, providing a steady Direct Current (DC) (Figure 6.4). In the field, batteries were my go-to for reliable power, essential when establishing communication lines in remote locations.

Transitioning, we step into the world of Alternating Current (AC) (Figure 6.5). Unlike batteries, AC changes direction periodically and is the form of electricity that powers our homes and bases. The ability to transform voltages easily makes AC versatile and vital for operating larger equipment and infrastructure.

Understanding the shift from batteries to AC is like adapting to different terrains in the field. Both have their unique characteristics, advantages, and applications, and knowing when and how to use them has been a game-changer in various situations throughout my service.

Laws & Logic
Ohm's Principles to Digital Circuitry

It's time to dive deep into the foundational laws and logic that govern the electronic world, from Ohm's principles to the intricacies of digital circuitry. Mastery of these concepts has been my north star, guiding me in troubleshooting and optimizing our equipment, keeping us one step ahead of our challenges.

We'll initiate our journey with Ohm's Law, a fundamental principle named after Georg Simon Ohm. It states that the current passing through a conductor between two points is directly proportional to the voltage across the two points and inversely proportional to the resistance between them. Grasping this principle was like learning the basics of marksmanship – it set the stage for accurate and effective engagements in the electronic field.

Advancing further, we delve into the realm of digital circuitry. This is where we transition from the analog to the digital, engaging with binary logic and gate functions that are the building blocks of computers and digital communications. Understanding digital circuitry was akin to deciphering a new tactical language, enabling seamless coordination and execution of complex tasks in the digital domain.

Becoming proficient in both Ohm's principles and digital circuitry is essential. These are the foundational elements that will empower you to understand, create, and troubleshoot electronic systems. I've relied on this knowledge to maintain operational efficiency, adapt to evolving scenarios, and ensure mission success, and so will you.

Wave & Wireless
The Radio Communication Chronicles

Future comrades! Let's gear up and ride the airwaves as we delve into the enthralling world of Wave & Wireless. This chapter is akin to learning the art of long-distance communication in the field – it's all about reaching out and staying connected, no matter the distance or terrain. First off, we'll tackle radio waves. These invisible yet powerful waves have been our lifeline in many missions. Imagine being in a dense forest or mountainous terrain; it's the radio waves that cut through the silence, connecting us to our base and fellow soldiers. Understanding their properties and how they propagate has been vital for me, ensuring clear and effective communication, even in the most challenging environments.

Next, we step into the realm of wireless communication. It's like learning the different dialects spoken across the units; each has its nuances, but the core message stays the same. We'll explore the diverse range of wireless technologies, from cellular networks to satellite communications. Learning the ins and outs of these technologies was a game-changer for me, enabling swift and secure communication, which is the backbone of any successful operation.

Toolbox Tour
Multimeters, Oscilloscopes, and Safety

Ready to take a guided tour through our electronic toolbox? We're diving into the essentials today – multimeters, oscilloscopes, and of course, safety. Believe me, knowing your way around these tools is like having a trusted sidearm; it's essential for keeping everything in check and running smoothly.

First on our tour is the multimeter. Think of this as your electronic Swiss Army knife; it measures voltage, current, and resistance. I've found myself reaching for this versatile tool in many field scenarios, diagnosing issues and ensuring our equipment was mission-ready. It's your go-to for a quick health check on any circuit.

Next, we encounter the oscilloscope. This piece of gear is like the tactical eyes of an electronic engineer. It visualizes the invisible, showing us how electrical signals change over time. In my years of service, using an oscilloscope has been pivotal for analyzing complex signals and getting to the root of tricky electronic problems.

Now, let's talk safety. In the field, your gear is only as good as your safety practices. It's the armor that keeps you and your equipment intact. We'll go over essential safety protocols, grounding practices, and protective gear. These are the guidelines I've followed to a tee, ensuring not just my safety, but the safety of my entire team.

The Final Salute
Alright, future service members, we're at the final stretch! It's time to gear up and get ready to conquer the EI Section. I'm here to share the tactics and strategies that have helped me, and countless others, turn challenges into triumphs. This is where your training meets the test, and I believe in your capability to achieve victory!

Why This Matters
In this chapter, you've unlocked the fundamentals of electronics, diving deep into the principles of electricity, circuitry, and the vital components that make modern technology tick. You've mastered the intricacies of currents and resistance, decoded the secrets of semiconductors like diodes and transistors, and explored the evolution of energy from batteries to alternating current. Additionally, you've become proficient with essential tools like multimeters and oscilloscopes, and learned crucial safety protocols. Each concept you've mastered here forms a solid foundation for both your ASVAB success and your future technical tasks in the military.

John's Final Words of Wisdom
As we navigate through this final stretch, keep in mind the strategies and knowledge we've built upon.

- **Hands-On Practice:** Regularly engage with electronic components and tools. Practical experience solidifies theoretical knowledge.

- **Think Critically:** Always approach problems methodically. Understanding the basics helps in troubleshooting complex issues.

- **Be Curious:** Never stop asking questions and exploring how things work. Curiosity drives innovation and mastery.

Having walked this path, I've seen firsthand how preparation and perseverance pave the way for success. You're not just gearing up for a test; you're fortifying your foundation for a rewarding journey in service.

Unit VII. AUTOMOTIVE AND SHOP INFORMATION (AS)

Dedicated future teammate! As we pivot into another paramount chapter, I'd like you to envision this section as a two-lane highway. On one side, we have the Auto Information (AI), the pulse of our vehicles and the intricacies that keep them roaring. On the other, we have the Shop Information (SI), the backbone of our maintenance and the craftsman's sanctuary. Both lanes, while distinct, are crucial, intertwining in the real world, ensuring our missions never stall. Having navigated both these terrains in my tenure, I can't stress their importance enough. There was a time, right in the thick of a desert mission, when understanding both the anatomy of our vehicle and the tools in our mobile shop proved vital. A sudden mechanical hitch could've cost us dearly. But with the know-how we're about to delve into, we were back on track in no time.

In the Auto Information stretch, our journey will cover:

- **Engine Exploration:** Unveiling the basics and the true heartbeat of autos.
- **Drive Dynamics:** A deep dive into the realms of transmission and braking.
- **Auto Anatomy:** Demystifying the suspension and electrical systems.
- **Engine Ecosystem:** The tales of cooling, lubrication, and the fuel story.
- **Tire Tales:** The saga of wheels, from birth to maintenance.
- **Guardian Gears:** Unraveling the safety protocols and emission checks.
- **Trouble Tracker:** The art of diagnosing those pesky auto dilemmas.

Switching lanes to Shop Information, we'll embark on:

- **Tool Time:** From basic hand tools to advanced machinery - know them all.
- **Material Mastery:** An exploration of metals, woods, and those crafty synthetics.
- **Joining Journeys:** The world of welding, soldering, and bonding.
- **Shop Safety:** The golden rules to avoid hazards and ensure protocol adherence.
- **Machinery Mechanics:** The know-how of operating and caring for common machines.
- **Blueprint Breakdown:** The skill of reading and interpreting crafty plans.
- **Measurement Methods:** Precision in sizing, scaling, and everything in between.

AUTO INFORMATION (AI)

In my 25 years of service, vehicles have often been more than just transport; they've been our lifeline, our shelter, and sometimes even the unsung heroes of our missions. I still fondly remember a challenging operation we had in rugged terrain. Our convoy faced an unexpected issue - and with a solid grasp of automotive knowledge, we not only diagnosed the problem but also fixed it on the spot, ensuring our mission's success. That's the practical power of understanding your vehicle.

Engine Exploration
Basics and the Heartbeat of Autos

The engine! Often referred to as the "heart" of any vehicle, it's what gives life to our metal companions. If you've ever been around car enthusiasts, you'd know that engine talk can easily ignite a passion. It's not just about horsepower and torque; it's about understanding the very core of what moves us – quite literally.

The Basics: What is an Engine?

An engine, in the context of our autos, is an internal combustion engine (ICE). In simple terms, it's a machine that converts fuel into mechanical energy, allowing our vehicles to move. At its heart lies a series of small explosions (combustions) that push pistons, turning the crankshaft, and eventually driving the wheels (Figure 7.1).

Parts of an Internal Combustion Car

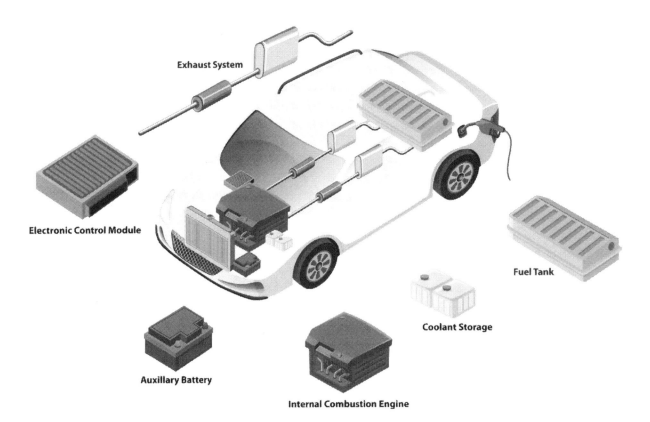

Figure 7.1: Important parts of a typical internal combustion engine in a car

Major Components:

Include (Figure 7.2):

- **Cylinders:** These are essentially the chambers where the magic happens. The fuel-air mixture is ignited, causing a rapid expansion of gases, which pushes a piston.

- **Pistons:** These metal rods move up and down within the cylinders due to the explosions. Their motion turns the crankshaft.

- **Crankshaft:** Connected to the pistons, the crankshaft rotates as the pistons move up and down, converting that up-and-down motion into rotational motion, eventually turning the wheels.

- **Camshaft:** This component plays a pivotal role in opening and closing engine valves, ensuring the right amount of air enters and exhaust gases leave the cylinders.

- **Timing Belt:** Responsible for keeping the movement of pistons and valves in sync, ensuring they don't collide.

- **Spark Plugs:** These igniters provide the spark necessary to ignite the fuel-air mixture within the cylinders.

- **Valves:** These control the intake of the air-fuel mixture and the exit of exhaust gases from the cylinders.

Parts of an Automobile Engine

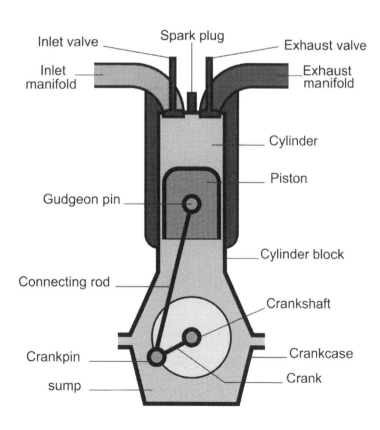

Figure 7.2: Working Schematic of an Automobile Engine

Engine Types:

There are various types of engines, including Inline, V-type, Boxer, etc. The differentiation is mainly based on the arrangement of cylinders. An Inline-4 (or I4) means there are 4 cylinders in a line, whereas a V6 means there are six cylinders arranged in a V shape.

Why Is Engine Knowledge Vital?

Understanding the engine is foundational, not just for this test but for real-world application. An efficient engine means better fuel consumption, lower emissions, and higher performance. In the field, when you're miles away from any workshop, grasping the basics can be the difference between being stranded and making it to your destination. Throughout my career, a basic comprehension of engines has saved me multiple times. I recall being in a tight spot once when our vehicle suddenly stuttered to a stop. A rudimentary understanding, paired with some hands-on tinkering, enabled us to address the minor hiccup swiftly. A little knowledge goes a long way!

Drive Dynamics
Delving into Transmission and Braking Realms

While the engine might be the heart of a vehicle, the transmission and brakes are its backbone and reflexes, respectively. These systems play crucial roles in making the vehicle move in the desired direction, changing gears, and stopping when required. It's akin to our human body: even if the heart pumps blood efficiently, we need our nerves and reflexes to act promptly. In this section, we'll take a deep dive into the world of transmission and braking.

Transmission 101: The Gear Genius

The primary purpose of a transmission system is to transmit power from the engine to the wheels. The process involves either upshifting to accelerate or downshifting to provide more power at lower speeds.

- **Manual Transmission:** Commonly referred to as a 'stick shift', this transmission type requires the driver to manually change gears using a clutch pedal and gear lever.
- **Automatic Transmission:** This system automatically changes gears as you accelerate or decelerate. It's generally more straightforward for beginners but offers less manual control.
- **Continuously Variable Transmission (CVT):** Unlike traditional transmissions with a set number of gears, CVTs use pulleys and belts, providing an almost infinite range of ratios.
- **Dual Clutch Transmission (DCT):** This system operates with two separate gear sets and clutches, making for faster gear shifts.

Braking Basics: The Science of Stopping

Just as crucial as the ability to move is the power to stop. The braking system plays a pivotal role in ensuring safety (Figure 7.3).

- **Disc Brakes:** These use a flat, round disc-shaped rotor, with brake pads applying pressure to either side of it. They're popular due to their efficient heat dissipation and strong stopping power.
- **Drum Brakes:** Older but still in use, these involve brake shoes pushing out against the inside of a brake drum to create friction and stop the vehicle.
- **Anti-lock Braking System (ABS):** This system prevents the wheels from locking up during braking, ensuring that the car doesn't skid, especially on slippery surfaces.

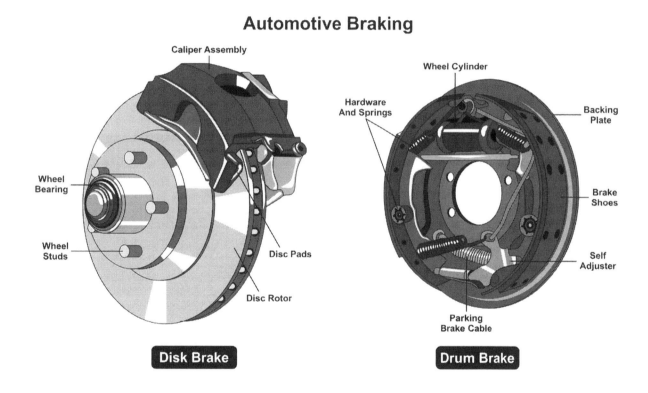

Figure 7.2: Working Schematic of an Automobile Engine

Why Understanding Drive Dynamics is Crucial?

A vehicle's performance, fuel efficiency, and safety depend heavily on its transmission and braking systems. In my years of experience, understanding these dynamics has often been the line between a safe maneuver and a potential mishap. I vividly remember a slippery road during one of our drills; having knowledge about the ABS system made all the difference in navigating that challenging terrain. In the vast world of automobiles, the more you know, the safer and more efficient your journey becomes. As we shift gears to further delve into the automotive realm, let's remember the importance of these drive dynamics and their role in our on-road journey.

Auto Anatomy

Suspension and Electrical Mysteries Unveiled

In the intricate dance of automotive machinery, two systems often leave many mystified: the suspension and electrical systems. These systems are the unsung heroes, ensuring your ride is smooth and your vehicle's functionalities are electrically orchestrated to perfection. Let's journey into these realms and unveil their mysteries.

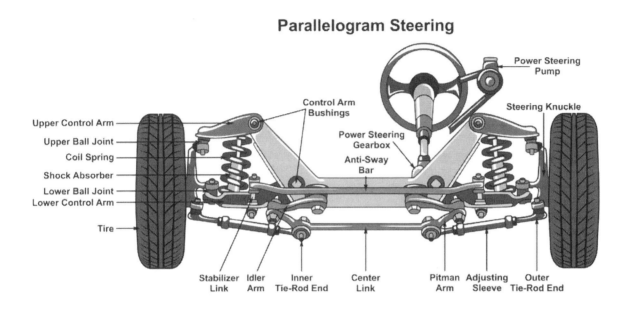

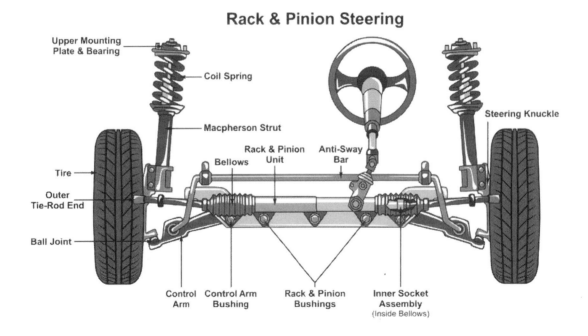

Figure 7.4: Working diagram and components of two different types of steering and suspension system.

Suspension Synergy: A Smooth Affair

Imagine driving over a rocky path or uneven terrain. It's the suspension system that ensures your ride remains as smooth as possible, absorbing the roughness and jolts (Figure 7.4).

- **Coil Springs:** These are the most common type of spring and work by absorbing shocks. When the vehicle goes over a bump, the spring compresses, absorbing the shock, and then expands back.
- **Leaf Springs:** Mostly found in older vehicles or trucks, these are layers of metal bound together to act as a singular spring unit.
- **Shock Absorbers:** Working alongside springs, shock absorbers dissipate the energy absorbed by the springs, ensuring there's no unwanted bouncing after a bump.
- **Struts:** A combination of spring and shock absorber into one unit. Struts provide structural support to the vehicle's suspension.

Electrifying Endeavors: Vehicle's Nervous System

Much like our body's nervous system, a vehicle's electrical system sends information and energy wherever needed, powering everything from your headlights to the radio (Figure 7.5).

- **Battery:** The heart of the electrical system. It provides the necessary power to start the engine and powers all electronic components when the engine isn't running.
- **Alternator:** Once the vehicle is running, the alternator takes over from the battery to power the vehicle's systems and also recharge the battery.
- **Starter Motor:** Draws electricity from the battery to start the engine.
- **Wiring and Fuses:** A complex network of wires carries power to various parts of the vehicle, with fuses acting as protective gatekeepers, preventing overloads.

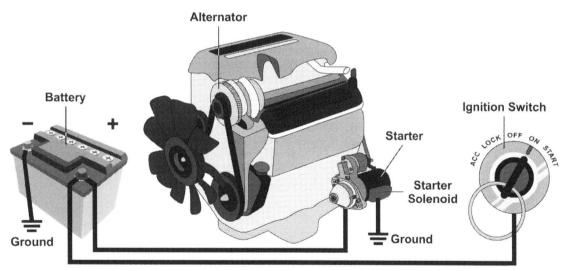

Figure 7.5: Engine Starting System of an Automobile.

The Harmony of Auto Anatomy

In my years serving in the military and working with various machinery, I've come to appreciate the brilliance of vehicle design. Our vehicles are an ensemble of well-coordinated systems, each playing its unique role. Understanding their functions not only fosters admiration for these but also empowers you with knowledge that can be pivotal during unexpected situations.

Engine Ecosystem
Cooling, Lubrication, and Fuel's Story

The engine, often heralded as the beating heart of a vehicle, requires a meticulous ecosystem to ensure its optimal function. Like the human body, it needs a cooling system to regulate its temperature, lubrication to prevent wear and tear, and fuel to function. Let's dive deeper into these critical systems, ensuring our engines hum along without a hitch.

Thermal Taming: The Cooling System
Engines produce significant heat when they operate. Without regulation, this heat could cause serious damage. Enter the cooling system (Figure 7.6).

- **Radiator:** The primary component responsible for cooling the engine. It circulates coolant, dissipating heat as the coolant passes through its coils.
- **Thermostat:** Regulates the flow of coolant based on the engine's temperature. It ensures the engine warms up quickly and then keeps it at a steady temperature.
- **Water Pump:** Drives the coolant from the radiator, through the engine, and back again, maintaining a continuous flow.
- **Coolant:** A specially formulated fluid that can absorb and transfer large amounts of heat without boiling.

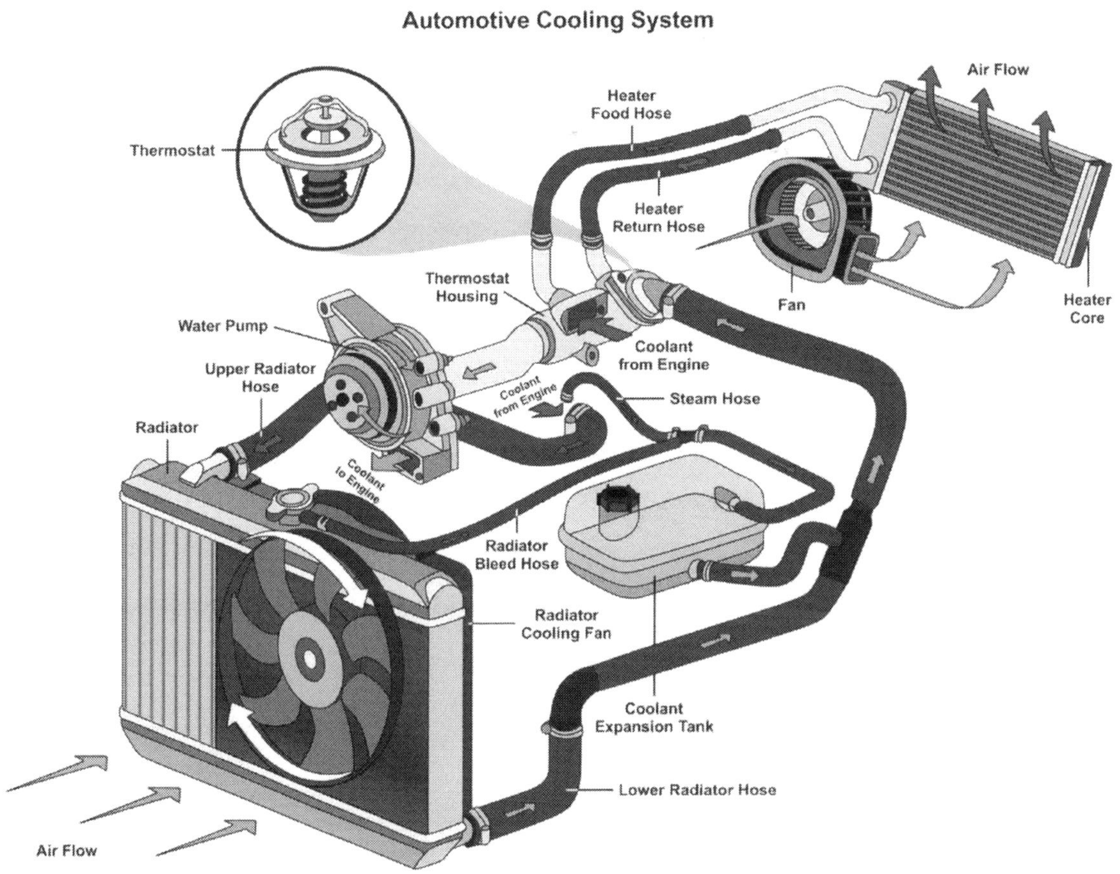

Figure 7.6: Cooling System of an Automobile

Silky Smooth: The Lubrication System

Friction is the age-old enemy of machinery. Within the engine, metal parts constantly move against each other, and without lubrication, they'd wear out rapidly (Figure 7.7).

- **Oil Pump:** Circulates oil throughout the engine.
- **Oil Filter:** As oil circulates, it picks up dirt and grit. The filter ensures these contaminants don't cause wear.
- **Oil Pan:** The reservoir holding the oil, located at the engine's bottom.
- **Lubricating Oil:** The lifeblood of the engine. Its primary purpose is to reduce friction between moving parts, but it also helps with cooling, sealing, and cleaning.

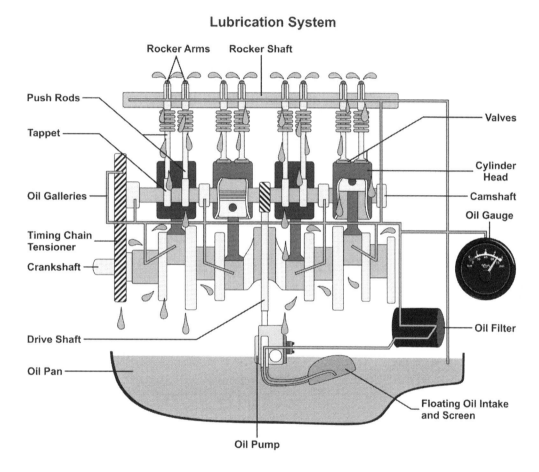

Figure 7.7: Lubrication System of an Automobile Engine

Fuel's Fantasia: Powering the Journey

Fuel is the energy source propelling our vehicles (Figure 7.8). Its intricate journey from the tank to combustion in the engine's cylinders is a tale of precision.

- **Fuel Tank:** The storage space for fuel.
- **Fuel Pump:** Transports fuel from the tank to the engine.
- **Fuel Filter:** Keeps impurities out, ensuring only clean fuel reaches the engine.
- **Fuel Injectors:** Precision instruments that spray fuel into the engine's combustion chambers in a fine mist, facilitating efficient combustion

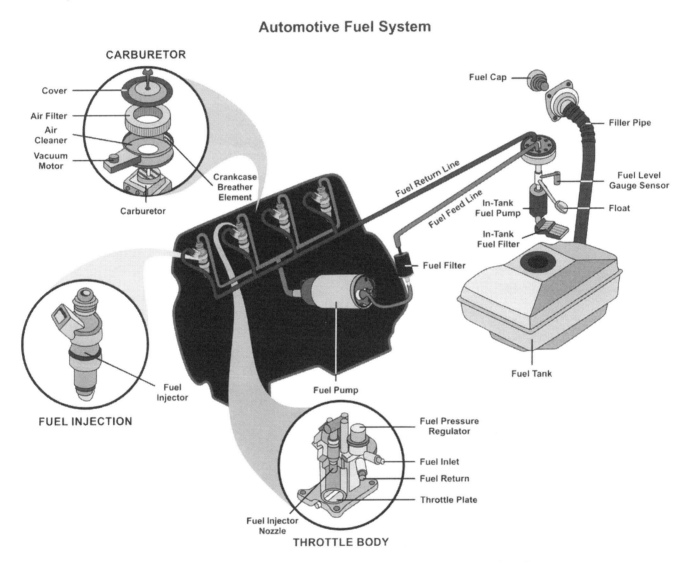

Figure 7.8: Complete Schematic Diagram of an Automobile Traction and Fuel System

Harmonious Symphony of the Engine

Back in my military days, I remember a particular convoy mission across a desert. The scorching heat was a true test for our vehicles' cooling systems. Proper lubrication ensured our engines didn't give out, and understanding our fuel system was vital in rationing our resources. That mission solidified my appreciation for the engine's delicate ecosystem. Understanding these systems is paramount. They work in harmony, ensuring our engines run smoothly, powerfully, and efficiently.

Tire Tales
The Journey of Wheels and Maintenance

In the realm of vehicles, if engines are the heart, then tires are most certainly the feet. They're our direct contact with the ground, affecting everything from the ride's comfort to the safety of our journeys. Let's journey down the winding road of tire tales, shedding light on their importance and the secrets behind their maintenance.

The Anatomy of a Tire
At first glance, a tire might seem simple – it's round, rubbery, and rolls. But the intricacies within are profound (Figure 7.9).

- **Tread:** The patterned outer surface of the tire that comes in contact with the road. Different patterns cater to varying conditions – rain, snow, off-road, etc.
- **Sidewall:** The side of the tire. It provides lateral stability and houses information about the tire – size, type, load capacity, and more.
- **Bead:** A steel wire encased in rubber. It ensures the tire stays attached securely to the wheel.
- **Ply:** Layers of fabric providing the structural strength to the tire. They're typically made of polyester, steel, or nylon.

Structure and Parts of the Tire

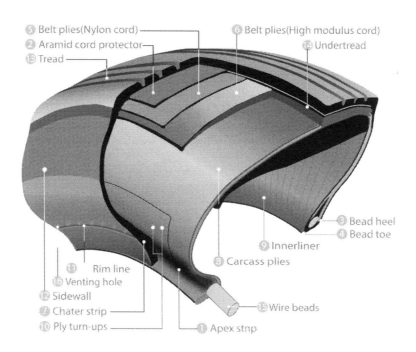

Figure 7.9: Cross-sectional view of a radial tire demonstrating its components.

Importance of Tire Maintenance

Like any component of a vehicle, tires require attention and care. Properly maintained tires can save you money, offer a smoother ride, and most importantly, keep you safe.

- **Tire Pressure:** A critical factor. Over or under-inflation can lead to uneven wear, decreased fuel efficiency, and even tire failure.
- **Rotation:** Regularly switching the position of your tires on the vehicle. This ensures even wear and can prolong the life of your tires.
- **Alignment and Balancing:** Ensures the tires wear evenly and the vehicle doesn't pull to one side.

Guardian Gears
Safety and Emission Protocols Deciphered

Ah, safety and emissions, the unsung heroes of our vehicular orchestra. If an automobile was a human body, these would be its immune system. They silently work in the background, protecting both the rider and the environment. Let's unveil the intricate dance of safety measures and emission standards in modern vehicles.

Auto Safety Measures

Today's vehicles come packed with features aiming to keep drivers, passengers, and even pedestrians safe. Here are a few worth highlighting:

- **Airbags:** Deployed during collisions, they cushion and protect passengers from injury.
- **Anti-lock Braking System (ABS):** Helps prevent wheel lock-up during emergency braking scenarios, allowing for more controlled stops.
- **Traction Control System (TCS):** Reduces wheel spin during acceleration by adjusting engine power or applying brake force to specific wheels.
- **Electronic Stability Control (ESC):** Improves a vehicle's stability by detecting and minimizing skids.

Personal Journey Down Memory Lane

I remember back in my early days, before my service, when I took my first long road trip. Somewhere along the interstate, I faced a tire blowout. Young and inexperienced, I'd overlooked the importance of tire pressure. That incident wasn't just a wake-up call, but it became a lesson I often shared with my buddies in the military, emphasizing the importance of routine checks and maintenance.

As we continue to navigate the vast world of automotive knowledge, remember that while engines provide power, it's the tires that translate that power into movement. They deserve our respect, care, and understanding. So, next time you hit the road, spare a thought for those four rubber wonders keeping you grounded and moving forward.

Emission Protocols: Clearing the Air

Protecting our environment is a shared responsibility. Vehicles, being significant contributors to air pollution, need stringent emission controls (Figure 7.10).

- **Catalytic Converters:** These devices reduce harmful pollutants by converting them into less harmful emissions before they leave the car's exhaust system.
- **Evaporative Emission Control (EVAP) System:** This prevents noxious gas build-ups and limits the escape of fuel vapors from the fuel system.
- **Exhaust Gas Recirculation (EGR):** This system reduces the amount of nitrogen oxide that gets released from the vehicle's engine, particularly at high temperatures.

Exhaust System

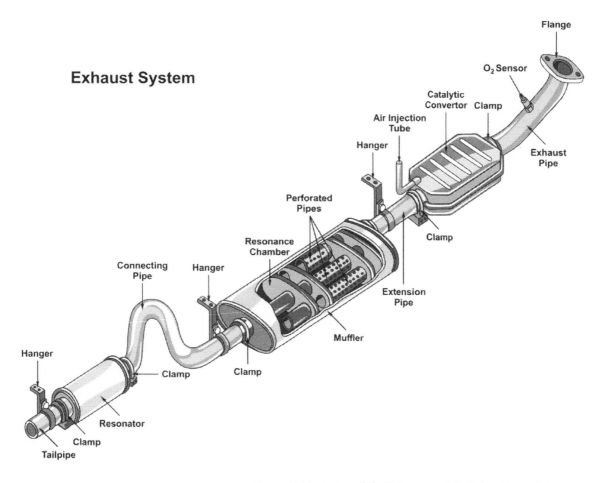

Figure 7.10: Automobile Exhaust-and-Emission Control System

Reflecting on Real-World Importance

Years ago, while stationed overseas, I remember a colleague who'd bought a vintage car. We loved that beauty! However, it was clear the car wasn't in line with modern emission standards. That old-timer belched smoke like a chimney! It was a real-world testament to how far we've come in our efforts to protect our environment, making me appreciate the importance of current emission controls.

Cars, trucks, and bikes aren't just about moving from point A to B; they play a role in our collective responsibility towards our world and its inhabitants. Understanding and respecting the intricate systems in place is not just about being a car enthusiast, but a steward of our planet.

Trouble Tracker
Diagnosing Common Auto Dilemmas

Anyone who's spent a good amount of time behind the wheel has faced a vehicle hiccup or two. It's an unavoidable rite of passage for any auto owner. Whether it's a weird rattle under the hood, a mysterious light flashing on your dashboard, or an unusual thump from the back, diagnosing these automotive conundrums is crucial for safe and efficient driving. Let's steer into some common problems and their likely culprits.

1. ***Engine Doesn't Start:***
   Include (Figure 7.11):

   - **Battery Issues:** One of the most common culprits. Dimmed dashboard lights when attempting to start can indicate a drained battery.
   - **Faulty Ignition Switch:** If turning the key doesn't start the engine but the battery seems to be functioning, the ignition switch might be at fault.
   - **Fuel Pump Issues:** A non-responsive fuel pump could mean the engine isn't getting the fuel it needs.

Figure 7.11: Different Types of indications in a typical car.

2. *Overheating Engine:*

- **Low Coolant Levels:** This is typically the prime suspect. Check the coolant reservoir.
- **Malfunctioning Thermostat:** A faulty thermostat can block the coolant flow.
- **Radiator Issues:** Leaks, blockages, or a failing radiator fan can cause the engine to overheat.

3. *Poor Fuel Economy:*

- **Dirty Air Filters:** A clogged filter can reduce fuel efficiency.
- **Malfunctioning Oxygen Sensors:** These sensors help regulate the air-to-fuel ratio. A faulty one can disrupt this balance.
- **Under-Inflated Tires:** Properly inflated tires can improve gas mileage by up to 3%.

4. *Brakes Squealing or Grinding:*

- **Worn-out Brake Pads:** Over time, brake pads wear down, leading to metal-on-metal contact.
- **Rusted Rotors:** If a car has been stationary for a long time, especially in damp conditions, rotors can rust.
- **Low-Quality Brake Pads:** Not all brake pads are created equal. Some might be noisier than others.

A Personal Anecdote for the Road:

I recall a time during a winter deployment when my vehicle started acting up. Amidst heavy snowfall, it wouldn't start. While my buddies and I were brainstorming solutions, a seasoned sergeant pointed out a frozen fuel line. His years of dealing with cars in cold climates came to our rescue. It was a practical lesson on the value of understanding common auto issues. In essence, a well-maintained car is like a trusted comrade: dependable, resilient, and there when you need it. Equip yourself with the knowledge to spot common issues, and you'll not only save time and money but also ensure the safety and longevity of your vehicle.

SHOP INFORMATION (SI)

Delving into the world of shop operations and mechanics isn't just about using tools; it's about understanding materials, grasping safety protocols, and mastering techniques. Whether you're a rookie trying to discern the difference between a Phillips and a flathead or an old hand ready to dive into the intricate realms of machinery mechanics, this section aims to gear you up with essential shop knowledge.

Tool Time
Understanding Basic and Advanced Tools

When I first started my hands-on training, I remember standing in front of a colossal tool wall, feeling a tad overwhelmed. Each tool had its own purpose, its own technique. Understanding and mastering them is akin to a pianist learning every key on the piano – integral to the performance. Whether you're just starting or looking to expand your skill set, getting a firm grip on your tools is paramount.

1. Basic Tools

- **Wrenches (Open-end, Box-end, Combination, Adjustable):** The wrench family is vast (Figure 7.12). While their core function is to turn bolts and nuts, each type is designed for specific tasks and accessibility. Open-end wrenches, for instance, offer a grip from the side, while box-end wrenches encircle a nut or bolt head entirely.

Figure 7.12: Different Types of Wrenches used for ensuring Mechanical Connections

- **Screwdrivers (Flathead, Phillips, Torx, Allen):** Another indispensable set. Their designs cater to specific screw heads, ensuring efficient and damage-free work. Flatheads are your typical slotted screwdrivers, while Phillips have a cross shape. Torx and Allen, on the other hand, are more specialized.

- **Pliers (Needle Nose, Channel Locks, Wire Cutters):** Pliers come in different shapes for various gripping, bending, or cutting tasks. Needle Nose pliers, for instance, are perfect for tight spaces or delicate work.

2. Advanced Tools

- **Power Drill & Bits:** A game-changer for any mechanic. Not only can it drill holes, but with various bits, it can also act as a powerful screwdriver or even a sander.

- **Oscilloscope:** This electronic test instrument allows technicians to view varying signal voltages. It's a must when delving into electronic diagnostics.

- **Digital Multimeter:** A staple in electrical diagnostics, the multimeter measures voltage, current, and resistance. Essential when pinpointing electrical issues or ensuring connections are sound.

Personal Insight:
Back in the day, I was working on a project, and the wrench just wouldn't fit. After a bit of struggle, a senior handed me an adjustable wrench, and the difference was night and day. It taught me that knowing your tools isn't just about efficiency; it's about making the impossible possible.

Take the time to familiarize yourself with each tool. Understand its application, its strengths, and its limitations. Like a trusted companion, they'll be by your side, ensuring your success every step of the way.

Material Mastery
Metals, Woods, and Synthetics

Walking into a shop, one can easily get lost amidst the vast array of materials available. Metals gleaming, woods emanating a fresh scent, and synthetics offering a colorful diversity. Each material has its own unique characteristics, and mastering them is crucial for any aspiring technician or craftsman. Let's break it down.

1. Metals

- **Ferrous Metals (e.g., Iron, Steel):** These are metals with iron as their primary component. Known for their strength and durability, ferrous metals are commonly used in construction, automotive, and countless other industries.

- **Non-Ferrous Metals (e.g., Copper, Aluminum, Brass):** Lacking significant iron content, these metals resist corrosion better and are lighter in weight. They're often employed in electrical works, aviation, and decorative arts.

2. Woods

- **Hardwoods (e.g., Oak, Maple, Walnut):** Derived from deciduous trees, hardwoods are dense and sturdy, making them ideal for furniture, flooring, and crafting fine objects.

- **Softwoods (e.g., Pine, Fir, Cedar):** Sourced from coniferous trees, softwoods are more pliable. They find their purpose in construction, paper creation, and some crafts.

3. Synthetics

- **Plastics & Polymers:** From toys to tools, plastics are everywhere. They're moldable, resistant to many chemicals, and come in myriad colors and flexibilities.
- **Composites (e.g., Fiberglass, Carbon Fiber):** When you merge two or more materials to get the best of their properties, you get composites. Think of boats, sports equipment, even aerospace applications.

Personal Insight:
I once embarked on a project requiring both metals and wood. The journey from sketching to sourcing the right materials, then melding them harmoniously, was a profound lesson. It highlighted the importance of not just knowing your materials, but respecting their individual strengths and weaknesses.

Remember, your result is often a direct reflection of the materials you choose. Select wisely, treat them with care, and they'll reward you with an impeccable finish.

Joining Journeys
Welding, Soldering, and Bonding

In the grand tapestry of craftsmanship, joining materials is an art and a science. It's like stitching fabric, but here, we're binding metals, plastics, or even woods. Let's explore the most common joining techniques and the nuances that come with each.

1. Welding
Welding is the process of fusing materials together, typically metals, by melting the parts and adding a filler, which solidifies to form a robust joint. There are various welding methods, including arc welding, gas welding, and even laser welding.

2. Soldering

Soldering is akin to welding but at a lower temperature. It involves melting a filler metal (or solder) into the joint between two workpieces. This is commonly employed in electronics to create electrical connections.

3. Bonding

Bonding is the technique of joining materials using adhesives. The range of adhesives available today is vast, with some designed for specific materials and conditions, from super glues for household use to specialized adhesives for aerospace applications.

Personal Insight:

I remember my first foray into welding back at the base. A fellow servicemember and I decided to fix a broken metal chair. Equipped with enthusiasm but limited knowledge, we ended up with a chair that was, well, not quite sit-worthy. This experience drove home the importance of mastering joining techniques. When done correctly, the joined pieces can often be stronger than the individual parts. In your journey through the realm of materials and their union, always prioritize safety. Proper gear, like welding helmets or safety glasses, is non-negotiable. Understand the materials, respect the tools, and always, always keep learning.

Shop Safety
Avoiding Hazards and Proper Protocols

Let me be clear from the outset: a shop, be it for auto or general crafts, can be both a sanctuary of creation and a hotspot for accidents. Over the years, I've seen that understanding and respecting shop safety protocols is the difference between efficient work and unfortunate mishaps. As a dedicated trainee or professional, your safety and the safety of those around you should always be paramount. Let's delve into the key considerations.

1. Personal Protective Equipment (PPE)

The cornerstone of safety is PPE. Depending on the task at hand, this might include safety goggles, ear protection, gloves, welding helmets, respirators, and protective clothing.

2. Tool Maintenance and Storage

A well-maintained tool is a safe tool. Regularly inspect your equipment for any wear or damage. Additionally, organize your workspace and ensure every tool has a designated storage spot. This not only helps in avoiding accidental injuries but also promotes efficiency.

3. Machine Guards

Machine guards are life-savers, literally. They are designed to protect the user from flying debris, moving parts, sparks, and more. Always ensure that guards are in place and functioning correctly.

4. Proper Ventilation

Especially in tasks like welding or working with chemicals, proper ventilation is crucial. It ensures you're not inhaling potentially hazardous fumes.

5. Fire Safety

Have firefighting equipment readily available and ensure you know how to use it. This includes fire extinguishers suited for different types of fires, fire blankets, and more.

6. First Aid and Emergency Procedures

Accidents, even with the best precautions, can happen. Ensure there's a first aid kit tailored for workshop accidents and that everyone is familiar with its contents and basic first aid procedures.

Personal Insight:

Years ago, during a routine task, a small oversight led to a minor but painful burn on my hand. The swift response of a colleague and the immediate availability of a first aid kit turned what could have been a severe injury into a manageable one. This incident was a stark reminder that safety protocols are not just guidelines;

they're the lifelines we rely on. In every task, remember this mantra: Safety first, always.

Machinery Mechanics
Operating and Maintaining Common Machines

The heart of any workshop, big or small, lies in its machines. These pieces of equipment amplify human effort, making tasks more efficient and outcomes more precise. However, with great power comes great responsibility. Proper operation and routine maintenance of these machines not only ensure longevity but also the safety of the operator. Let's dive into the world of machinery mechanics.

1. **Understand the Machine Manual**
   Before operating any machine, thoroughly familiarize yourself with its manual. This booklet, often overlooked, contains a wealth of information including the machine's operational guidelines, safety precautions, and maintenance tips.

2. **Routine Inspections**
   Before every use, conduct a brief inspection of the machine. Check for any visible damage, loose parts, or signs of wear. This habit can avert potential breakdowns and accidents.

3. **Regular Maintenance**
   Just like our cars, machines also require routine maintenance. Whether it's lubricating moving parts, replacing worn-out components, or calibrating for precision, scheduled maintenance is crucial.

4. **Safe Operation Protocols**
   Each machine has its own set of operational guidelines. Always adhere to them. This might include wearing specific PPE, maintaining a safe distance, or not operating certain machines in tandem.

5. **Training and Skill Development**
   Regularly update your skills. Attend workshops, training sessions, or simply engage in discussions with fellow operators. Sharing knowledge and ex-

periences can lead to enhanced safety and operational efficiency.

6. **Machine Storage**
   If a machine isn't in use, ensure it's stored correctly. Protect it from elements like moisture and dust, and disconnect it from the power source.

Personal Insight:
Back in my early days, I remember working alongside a seasoned machinist named Pete. One day, I casually commented on how meticulously he maintained his machines. With a wink, Pete replied, "Take care of your machines, and they'll take care of you." Over the years, this simple advice has not only saved me from countless machine breakdowns but also from potential accidents.

Blueprint Breakdown
Reading and Interpreting Plans

Blueprints, often regarded as the "maps" of the construction and manufacturing world, carry detailed guidelines for building or producing just about anything. From colossal skyscrapers to the most intricate of tools, a well-drafted blueprint ensures that everyone involved is on the same page, literally and figuratively. For someone working in a shop or involved in construction, understanding how to read these documents is invaluable. Let's delve into the art and science of interpreting blueprints.

1. **Introduction to Blueprints**
   Blueprints are detailed technical drawings that communicate how something is to be made or built. They can be as straightforward as a diagram of a tool or as complex as the architectural plans for a multi-story building.

2. **The Language of Symbols**
   Blueprints have their own language, made up of symbols and abbreviations. Each symbol, be it for electrical outlets, machinery parts, or welding joints, has a specific meaning that standardizes the blueprint across industries.

3. Scales and Dimensions

Always pay attention to the scale mentioned in the blueprint. This ensures that your output matches the desired size and proportions. Dimensions guide the size, length, breadth, and depth of the item or structure.

4. Views and Perspectives

Blueprints present multiple views – top view, side view, cross-sectional view, etc., to provide a comprehensive understanding of the subject. Grasping the perspective aids in accurate construction or manufacturing.

5. Material and Specification Lists

Often, blueprints will come with lists specifying the materials to be used or the standards to be adhered to. These lists are pivotal for ensuring quality and longevity.

6. Revisions and Updates

Blueprints can undergo revisions. Always ensure you're working with the most updated version, and be mindful of any notes or changes highlighted.

Personal Insight:

During my engineering days, I once mistakenly built a model based on an outdated blueprint. The hours of effort felt wasted, but it taught me a lifelong lesson: Always double-check. Blueprints are more than just sheets of paper; they are comprehensive guides that, when read correctly, lead to beautiful, functional, and safe creations.

Measurement Methods
Accurate Sizing and Scaling

Accurate measurements are the bedrock of any successful project. Whether you're designing a furniture piece, fabricating a machine component, or setting up a workshop layout, precision in sizing and scaling is paramount. A mere millimeter off can compromise the entire functionality or safety of an assembly. Let's navigate the realm of measurement methods, ensuring

that what gets envisioned gets actualized with precision.

1. Introduction to Measurement

Measurement is the assignment of a number to a characteristic of an object, based on some standard or convention. In a workshop or manufacturing scenario, it's the accurate determination of sizes, distances, or quantities.

2. Tools of the Trade

There's an array of tools available, tailored for different needs:

- **Rulers and Measuring Tapes:** For linear measurements.
- **Calipers:** For precise internal and external distances.
- **Micrometers:** Offering even higher precision than calipers.
- **Protractors:** For measuring angles.
- **Gauges:** To determine diameters or thicknesses.

3. The Importance of Units

Always be clear about the unit of measurement. Whether it's inches, centimeters, or a more specialized unit, consistency is key. Convert measurements when needed but always double-check for accuracy.

4. Digital vs. Manual Measurements

The digital age has ushered in tools that provide readouts electronically, like digital calipers or laser distance measurers. While they offer convenience and often more precision, manual tools still have their place, especially where tactile feedback is important.

5. Calibration and Maintenance

Just like any tool, your measuring devices need care. Regular calibration ensures they provide accurate readings. Protect them from physical damage and environmental factors that could affect their precision.

6. Tolerances

In many projects, a slight deviation from the intended measurement is acceptable, known as tolerance. However, understanding and respecting the defined tolerances is crucial, especially in components that interface with others.

Personal Insight:

Years ago, while crafting a custom shelf, I miscalculated by a mere half-inch. Though it might seem minuscule, it resulted in an uneven alignment that haunted my perfectionist spirit. That day taught me the value of meticulous measuring. Remember, in the world of creation, precision is not just a need; it's an art.

The Final Salute

You've just conquered the intricacies of Automotive and Shop Information, proving your mettle in both practical and theoretical aspects. From engine dynamics to mastering essential tools, your knowledge now spans the crucial details that keep operations running smoothly. Keep this knowledge sharp; it's your key to solving real-world challenges efficiently.

What We've Achieved

In this chapter, you've navigated the dual lanes of Auto Information and Shop Information, mastering the essentials that make our mechanical world tick. You've explored the heart of vehicles, understanding engines, transmissions, and braking systems, while also delving into the nuances of suspension and electrical systems. On the shop side, you've become proficient with a variety of tools, learned the importance of different materials, and grasped the art of joining methods like welding and soldering. Each topic has armed you with the skills to diagnose issues, perform maintenance, and ensure safety in every mechanical endeavor.

Why This Matters

In the vast domain of automotive and shop knowledge, every intricate detail counts. From the heartbeats of engines to the whisper of machinery, the symphony of accurate measurements to the dance of welding sparks, mastering each facet ensures both safety and excellence. As we journey together through the realms of autos and shops, it's evident that success lies in understanding and respecting each component's role. Whether you're a budding mechanic, an aspiring engineer, or a curious enthusiast, remember: a well-equipped mind is the most valuable tool in any workshop. As always, may your endeavors be guided by knowledge and executed with precision.

John's Final Words of Wisdom

Get Your Hands Dirty: Dive into real projects and use your newfound skills. Practical application turns knowledge into expertise.

- **Stay Updated:** Keep abreast of the latest automotive and shop technologies. Innovation never stops.

- **Think Safety First:** Always prioritize safety protocols. A safe environment is a productive one.

- **Keep Exploring:** Never stop learning about new tools, techniques, and materials. Curiosity drives expertise.

Great job, team! Your skills in automotive and shop information are now a vital part of your toolkit. Keep pushing forward!

Unit VIII. MECHANICAL COMPREHENSION (MC)

Buckle up, as we're about to embark on the Mechanical Comprehension journey, a critical segment of the ASVAB that's not just about understanding the principles of mechanics but visualizing and applying them. This section is your opportunity to demonstrate a grasp of physical concepts and mechanical reasoning, which are not just academic exercises but vital skills that could shape your role in the military. We'll delve into the heart of physics, exploring forces, energy, machines, and properties of materials. Think of it as learning the language of the physical world. These concepts are the very gears that keep the military machine running smoothly, from aircraft maintenance to combat engineering. My aim is to not only prepare you for the test ahead but to lay down a solid foundation for your future role in safeguarding our nation.

PHYSICS FUNDAMENTALS

Physics Primer & Movement Mechanics
Forces, Motion, and Levers

Forces: The Invisible Hands That Move Our World
In the military, forces are the unspoken commands that dictate every movement, whether it's a soldier marching, a jet taking off, or a ship sailing. A force is essentially a push or a pull upon an object resulting from its interaction with another object. It's what we calculate when we plan the trajectory of a projectile or when we must breach a barricade. It's measured in Newtons (N), and understanding its vector nature—how it has both magnitude and direction—is crucial.

Every operation we conduct is a study in balance—forces in equilibrium mean our bridges hold, our structures stand, and our formations maintain their integrity. But when forces are unbalanced, we witness acceleration or change in motion. Grasping this principle prepares you to predict the outcomes of these interactions, essential in both combat strategy and engineering tasks.

Motion: The Rhythm of Military Precision
Motion is movement, and in the armed forces, it's orchestrated with precision and intention. It's a concept that can be described by Newton's three laws, which I assure you, are just as relevant on the battlefield as in any physics classroom.

- **Newton's First Law (Law of Inertia):** A soldier remains at rest or marches at a constant speed in a straight line unless acted upon by an unbalanced force. It's the reason why a tank keeps moving unless something stops it.

- **Newton's Second Law (Law of Acceleration):** Acceleration of an object depends on the mass of the object and the amount of force applied. This principle lets us calculate how much thrust a jet engine needs to lift off based on the jet's mass and the force of gravity.

- **Newton's Third Law (Law of Action and Reaction):** For every action, there's an equal and opposite reaction. It's why a rifle recoils when it's fired. Understanding this helps us brace and adapt to these reactions.

Levers: The Simple Machines of Tactical Advantage

Levers are simple machines that give us a mechanical advantage, and in the military, they're everywhere. From the way a helicopter's control stick operates to the use of a crowbar to open heavy crates of supplies, levers amplify our strength. There are three classes of levers, differentiated by the placement of the fulcrum, load, and effort:

- **First-Class Lever:** Like a seesaw, the fulcrum is between the effort and the load. This type is about balance and precision—much like positioning a sniper for an optimal shot.

- **Second-Class Lever:** Such as a wheelbarrow, the load is between the fulcrum and the effort. It allows for moving heavier weights, akin to relocating heavy artillery with minimal force.

- **Third-Class Lever:** The effort is between the fulcrum and the load, like in a pair of tweezers. This setup is not about moving heavy loads but rather about precision and control—critical when defusing a device or administering first aid.

Understanding these concepts provides the mechanical comprehension needed to visualize and solve problems effectively, a skill that could be the difference between mission success and failure. As you master these principles, you're not only preparing to ace the ASVAB; you're gearing up to be a more effective and knowledgeable service member.

Rotational Realities
Wheels, Axles, and Pulleys

Wheels: The Round Revolution of Mobility

Wheels are central to nearly all land-based military operations, from the humvee patrolling rugged terrains to the transport aircraft landing gear that withstands the impact of rapid descents. A wheel reduces friction and makes it easier to move heavy objects—a basic concept with profound implications.

For instance, the wheels on an armored vehicle distribute the weight over a larger area, allowing for easier movement across challenging landscapes. Additionally, the size of the wheel in relation to the axle can be crucial; a larger wheel can roll over obstacles more easily, which is a principle applied when designing vehicles for maximum terrain adaptability.

Axles: The Central Shaft of Control

Axles serve as the central shaft for wheels to rotate around and can be found in almost every military vehicle. The design and function of axles are critical for maneuverability and control. In many military applications, axles are designed to provide power to the wheels, like in all-wheel-drive vehicles, enabling them to traverse difficult terrains.

In engineering terms, the axle must support the weight of the vehicle plus any cargo, endure the stresses of motion, and resist bending or breaking. When considering the physics, the torque applied through the axle translates into the wheel's rotational force, a concept exploited to create military vehicles that can accelerate quickly despite their heavy armaments.

Pulleys: The Lift and Advantage Systems

Pulleys are used in the military not just for lifting heavy loads, but also for redirecting forces and controlling equipment. A pulley system can be as simple as a single wheel with a rope to lift supplies or as complex as the systems used in aircraft carriers to assist in launching aircraft.

A single fixed pulley changes the direction of the force applied, allowing for more strategic positioning of personnel when moving objects. Meanwhile, a system of pulleys, or a block and tackle, can significantly reduce the effort needed to lift heavy equipment—a vital attribute when time and energy are of the essence during deployment operations.

Understanding the interplay of wheels, axles, and pulleys provides a fundamental appreciation for the mechanical ingenuity embedded in military hardware.

These elements are applied in various contexts to optimize the efficiency of military logistics, from the design of transport mechanisms to the setup of field equipment. Mastery of these mechanical principles not only ensures readiness for the ASVAB mechanical comprehension section but also equips you with the knowledge to envision and perhaps innovate the next generation of military machinery.

Fluid Dynamics
Hydraulics and Pneumatics Uncovered

Hydraulics: The Power of Liquids at Work
In the military realm, hydraulics play a pivotal role, with their application being found in a variety of systems from the recoil mechanisms of artillery to the control surfaces of an aircraft. The basic principle of hydraulics is simple: force applied at one point is transmitted to another point using an incompressible fluid, typically oil. The advantage lies in the multiplication of force; a small, manageable input force can be transformed into a large output force, making heavy lifting and precise movements achievable with relative ease.

Consider the hydraulic system in a military transport aircraft's landing gear. The compactness of the hydraulic machinery allows for heavy machinery to be operated within the limited space available, demonstrating hydraulics' invaluable nature in achieving high power density.

Pneumatics: The Force of Air
Pneumatics, on the other hand, deals with the use of gas, usually air, under pressure. The pneumatic systems are essential in various military applications such as missile launch systems or opening and closing the hatches of tanks or armored vehicles. These systems capitalize on the compressibility of gases; when compressed, gases exert force on the walls of their container, and this force can be harnessed to perform work.

For example, the pneumatic tools used in a military workshop for repairing vehicles utilize the high-speed air to drive bolts and fasteners quickly and with high precision. Moreover, the simplicity of design and the cleanliness of air as a resource make pneumatics a preferred choice for many operations where hydraulic fluid leaks could be detrimental.

Both hydraulics and pneumatics highlight the principle of Pascal's law, which states that pressure applied to a confined fluid is transmitted undiminished in all directions. Understanding the intricacies of these fluid systems is essential for any service member involved in the maintenance and operation of military technology. The principles of fluid dynamics, when harnessed through hydraulics and pneumatics, demonstrate the sophistication of modern military equipment and the ingenuity behind their operational capabilities.

Thermal Insights
Heat and Energy Transfers

The Transfer of Thermal Energy
Heat transfer is an essential concept in both civilian and military engineering applications, playing a critical role in everything from vehicle engine efficiency to the thermal imaging used for surveillance. There are three primary mechanisms of heat transfer: conduction, convection, and radiation.

Conduction: The Direct Heat Highway
Conduction is the process by which heat energy is transmitted through collisions between neighboring atoms or molecules. In the field, this principle is at work in the heat sinks of electronic systems. These are often used in military computers and communication devices to dissipate the heat generated by electronic components, preventing overheating and ensuring operational integrity.

Convection: Fluids in Motion
Convection occurs when heat is carried away by the movement of fluids, which can be either liquid or gas. Military vehicles often rely on convection cooling systems; for example, the radiator in a tank uses convection to transfer heat away from the engine, using a circulating fluid that moves heat to a cooler area where it can dissipate.

Radiation: Energy on the Move

Radiation is the transfer of heat through electromagnetic waves. It's a principle that can be observed in the heat signature of jets and vehicles, which military technologies such as infrared sensors and night-vision equipment detect. Understanding these signatures is crucial for both camouflage measures and the identification of friend or foe in combat scenarios.

Heat and Energy in Military Operations

In a military context, mastering the principles of heat and energy transfers is not only about understanding the functionality of equipment but also about survival and efficiency. For example, the design of a forward operating base must consider insulation and heat management for energy conservation and to maintain a low thermal profile, making it less detectable to enemy surveillance.

The knowledge of heat transfer mechanisms also underpins the development of advanced materials and clothing designed to regulate body temperature in various climates, critical for soldier comfort and performance. The application of heat and energy transfer principles is extensive and provides an essential foundation for many of the technical tasks and problem-solving situations that military personnel may encounter.

Mechanical Mechanisms
Gears, Devices, and Everyday Machinery

Gears: The Muscle of Machinery

Gears are ubiquitous in both civilian life and military machinery, serving as the fundamental building blocks of many mechanical systems. They work by transmitting torque through teeth with impressive precision and can be found in everything from wristwatches to aircraft carriers. In military technology, gears are central to the operation of weapon systems, enabling the precise aiming and firing mechanisms that are critical for both offensive and defensive operations.

Types of Gears and Their Uses

There are several types of gears, each with unique applications:

- **Spur Gears:** Used for their simplicity and efficiency in transmitting motion and power between parallel shafts.

- **Helical Gears:** Offer a smoother operation than spur gears and are commonly used in automotive transmissions.

- **Bevel Gears:** Have conically shaped teeth and are employed when the direction of a shaft's rotation needs to be changed.

- **Worm Gears:** Allow for large gear reductions and are used in systems where space is limited and a large gear reduction is needed in a single stage.

Devices: From Simple to Complex

Simple devices such as pulleys and wedges are the foundation of many complex machines. Pulleys can change the direction of applied force and are integral to systems like the block and tackle, which are used to lift heavy equipment in logistics operations. Wedges, another simple machine, transform a force applied to their blunt end into forces perpendicular to their inclined surfaces, a principle that is vital in the design of blades and cutting devices used in combat and survival situations.

Everyday Machinery in Military Applications

The everyday machinery that civilians take for granted often has enhanced, rugged counterparts in the military. For example:

- **Pumps:** Essential for moving fluids and are used in various military applications, from fueling aircraft to operating hydraulic systems in armored vehicles.

- **Compressors:** Used in everything from jet engines to refrigeration systems on naval ships.

- **Internal Combustion Engines:** Power a majority of military land vehicles and are prized for their reliability and power.

Understanding Machinery for the ASVAB

For ASVAB preparation, a clear understanding of gears and simple mechanical devices is crucial. It's not just about being able to recognize these components but also understanding how they work together to create efficient systems that can perform a wide range of functions. This knowledge will be assessed in the Mechanical Comprehension Section, which evaluates an individual's grasp of basic mechanical principles and their application in real-world scenarios.

Safety in Mechanics
Guarding Against Mishaps

The Premise of Safety

Safety in mechanics is a paramount concern that transcends all fields, from civilian garages to military maintenance hangars. It is the protective shield that guards individuals against the myriad of hazards present in mechanical environments. Establishing a comprehensive understanding of safety procedures and practices is not just about individual protection; it's about ensuring a functional and effective team in any setting.

Identifying Hazards

The first step to safety is recognizing potential dangers:

- **Mechanical Hazards:** involve moving parts, sharp edges, or hot surfaces that can cut, crush, or burn.

- **Chemical Hazards:** include exposures to harmful substances that can cause burns, poisoning, or long-term health issues.

- **Electrical Hazards:** involve the risk of shock, arc flash, or fire from improper handling of electrical components or systems.

Protective Measures

- **Personal Protective Equipment (PPE):** Utilizing helmets, gloves, goggles, and ear protection to shield against specific threats.

- **Safety Protocols:** Adhering to established guidelines for operating machinery, handling hazardous materials, and performing tasks like lockout-tagout to ensure machinery is properly shut down before maintenance.

- **Emergency Procedures:** Knowing the immediate steps to take in the event of an accident, such as spill containment, first aid, or equipment shutdown.

Maintenance and Training

- **Regular Equipment Checks:** Preventative maintenance is a critical safety aspect, ensuring that machinery is in top working condition and reducing the risk of malfunctions.

- **Training and Education:** Continuous education on the latest safety practices and the operation of new machinery is essential for keeping skills sharp and awareness high.

Military Applications

In the military, safety is not just about personal well-being; it is integral to mission success. Proper safety measures ensure:

- **Operational Readiness:** Equipment and personnel are always ready for deployment without delay due to injury or equipment failure.

- **Longevity of Service:** By preventing accidents and injuries, service members can have prolonged, productive careers.

- **Resource Preservation:** Protecting equipment from damage means valuable resources are not wasted on avoidable repairs or replacements

ASVAB Considerations

For the ASVAB, understanding safety in mechanics includes knowledge of common hazards, safety equipment, and safe practices. It is critical for potential service members to show that they can not only operate and understand machinery but also do so safely, preserving both their well-being and that of their unit.

The Final Salute

As you turn the page from this chapter to the next, carry forward the insights gained here. Remember that each mechanical concept you've grasped serves as a tool in your intellectual arsenal, a component in your problem-solving toolkit. Whether you apply these concepts in the engine room of a naval ship, the maintenance bay of a military base, or in the civilian world, the mechanical comprehension you develop today lays the groundwork for the innovations of tomorrow.

What We've Achieved

The Mechanical Comprehension chapter provides a comprehensive exploration of the principles that govern the physical world and the machinery operating within it. From the simple leverage afforded by a crowbar to the complex hydraulics of an aircraft's landing gear, these principles form the bedrock upon which modern technology stands.

Why This Matters

For the aspirants of the ASVAB and potential service members, mastering mechanical comprehension is not solely for academic achievement but for practical application in a variety of military and civilian roles. It equips you with the knowledge to tackle real-world problems, foresee the behavior of mechanical systems, and devise innovative solutions on the spot.

Understanding forces, motion, levers, and the intricate dance of gears and pulleys is crucial. Fluid dynamics unfurl the mysteries of hydraulics and pneumatics, while the study of heat and energy transfers lends insight into the conservation and efficiency of power in military machinery. Knowledge of safety in mechanics is the final, critical component that ensures these operations are conducted without harm to personnel or equipment.

John's Final Words of Wisdom

- **Embrace Curiosity:** Dive deep into understanding how things work. Your curiosity will drive your expertise and keep you engaged.

- **Practice Visualization:** Picture mechanical processes in your mind. This will enhance your ability to troubleshoot and innovate.

- **Collaborate and Learn:** Work with others to solve problems and share insights. Teamwork can offer new perspectives and accelerate learning.

- **Focus on Fundamentals:** Strong basics make tackling complex problems easier. Keep reinforcing foundational concepts.

Armed with this knowledge, you stand ready to advance not just in your ASVAB scoring but in your future endeavors where mechanical wisdom becomes the cornerstone of your success.

Unit IX. ASSEMBLING OBJECTS (AO)

The Assembling Objects (AO) category of ASVAB is a unique section that measures spatial abilities — an essential skill for potential service members. In this chapter, we will delve into the intricate world of spatial reasoning and object assembly, critical for roles where visualizing and manipulating objects in space is a daily task. Whether for technical positions, engineering roles, or combat situations, the ability to think in three dimensions translates into real-world problem-solving capabilities. Through a series of engaging exercises and detailed explanations, we will break down the fundamental concepts of spatial awareness, shape recognition, and the mental rotation of objects. You will learn to discern how separate components fit together to form a whole and how these skills apply to a multitude of tasks, from interpreting technical diagrams to assembling intricate equipment. Moreover, this section isn't just about fitting shapes into a given space; it's about visualizing outcomes, understanding the interplay between different components, and grasping the tangible aspects of abstract concepts. As we progress, we'll connect these skills with real-life applications in the military, where strategic assembly and disassembly often underpin mission success. By the end of this chapter, you will not only be better prepared for the Assembling Objects section of the ASVAB but also more adept at tackling spatial challenges in both military and civilian spheres. So, let's embark on this three-dimensional journey, where your cognitive maps will expand, and your ability to perceive, understand, and manipulate the physical world will grow exponentially.

ASSEMBLY SKILLS

Perspective & Assembly Foundations
Seeing Angles and Joining Basics

Understanding Perspective
Perspective is the lens through which we view the world, and in the realm of assembling objects, it is paramount. It allows us to interpret two-dimensional drawings or diagrams and visualize them as three-dimensional objects. This skill is vital in many military roles, such as when a pilot interprets a heads-up display or a technician reads schematics for equipment repair.

To master perspective,
one must understand the concepts of:

- **Horizon Line:** The distant point where the sky appears to meet the ground, anchoring the perspective.

- **Vanishing Points:** Points on the horizon line where parallel lines seem to converge, giving a sense of depth.

- **Plane:** The flat surface on which the objects rest. In a drawing, it's how we represent three-dimensional depth on a two-dimensional medium.

Assembly Basics
Joining basics, on the other hand, is about understanding how parts connect and interact. It's crucial for anyone who deals with the assembly or disassembly of objects, from loading munitions to constructing temporary barracks.

Key concepts include:

- **Interlocking:** Similar to puzzle pieces, interlocking involves connecting components that have complementary shapes.

- **Adjoining:** This is the simple side-by-side connection of parts, which may not be secure without additional fastening methods.

- **Fastening:** Utilizing various devices such as screws, bolts, or clips to secure parts together.

Practical Military Applications

In a practical military context, perspective and assembly skills are exercised daily:

- **Field Assembly:** Soldiers often have to quickly assemble and disassemble gear, weapons, or shelters. Accurately understanding how the pieces fit together is crucial.

- **Maintenance and Repair:** Technical roles require interpreting diagrams and blueprints to maintain and repair sophisticated equipment.

- **Load Planning:** When loading cargo or planning missions, it's necessary to understand how items will fit in a given space, which is a direct application of perspective and assembly skills.

ASVAB Focus

For the ASVAB, focusing on perspective and assembly foundations will enhance your spatial reasoning skills. You'll be presented with tasks that require you to mentally manipulate and combine various parts, assessing your aptitude for technical roles that involve spatial comprehension.

As an ASVAB expert with 25 years of experience in the field and specializing in ASVAB test preparation, I can provide an in-depth perspective on the Assembling Objects subtest, a critical component of the CAT-ASVAB. This subtest is meticulously designed to evaluate candidates' spatial abilities, a skill set that is not only essential for academic and occupational success but also vital for everyday tasks. It involves understanding and interpreting spatial relationships, fundamental in fields such as engineering, architecture, and various technical domains. Spatial skills enable individuals to effectively navigate and understand maps, architectural plans, technical drawings, and even medical imaging like X-rays.

In the Assembling Objects subtest, candidates are presented with 15 graphical problems that they need to solve within a stipulated time of 22 minutes. However, there's an alternate version of the test which includes tryout questions, as detailed in Chapter 1 of the preparatory material. In this version, the test extends to 42 minutes, encompassing 30 questions. This format is slightly different in the paper version of the ASVAB, where candidates face 25 questions with a time constraint of 15 minutes. This effectively means that each question needs to be solved in less than a minute. While this may seem daunting, it's quite manageable for those who are adept at solving jigsaw puzzles or have honed their spatial reasoning skills.

Over the years, I've observed a growing demand for professionals with robust spatial abilities. Industries are increasingly seeking individuals who can adeptly interpret complex graphical information such as graphs, maps, and technical drawings. This trend underscores the importance of the Assembling Objects subtest in the ASVAB.

To excel in this subtest, I recommend candidates engage regularly in activities that enhance spatial reasoning, like puzzle-solving, playing spatially oriented games, or even indulging in hobbies that require spatial visualization, such as model building. Moreover, familiarizing oneself with the test format and practicing with similar graphical problems can significantly boost performance.

Types of Questions Related to the
Assembling Objects Category

The Assembling Objects subtest of the ASVAB features specific types of questions designed to assess spatial reasoning abilities. This subtest is unique in its focus on visualizing how different parts can be combined to form a whole object. Here are the typical types of questions you can expect in this section:

- **Puzzle Questions:** Candidates are presented with various pieces of an object, like a jigsaw puzzle, and must determine how these pieces fit together to form a complete object. The key challenge is to visualize the end product and understand how each piece contributes to the overall structure.

The figure below represents this type of question (Figure 9.1). By looking closely at the given options, only option A can be selected as the answer to the question as the pieces fit perfectly together to make the shape given in the first image.

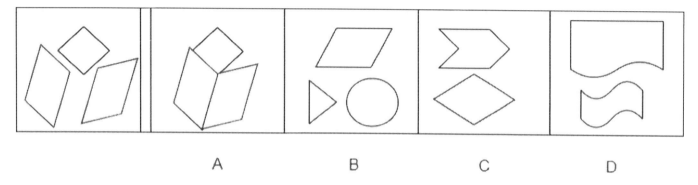

A   B   C   D

Figure 9.1: Example of a Puzzle Question

- **Rotational Questions:** Candidates are required to mentally rotate objects or parts of an object. You might be shown an object in a particular orientation and asked to identify what it would look like if rotated to a different angle. This tests your ability to maintain spatial relationships in your mind while an object is being manipulated.
- **Mirror Image Questions:** These involve identifying the mirror image of a given object or assembly. It requires an understanding of symmetry and the ability to mentally flip objects across an axis.
- **Combination Questions:** Sometimes, you'll encounter questions that require you to combine two or more of the above skills. For example, you might need to first rotate a piece and then determine how it fits into a puzzle.

This type of question is represented by the following figure (Figure 9.2).

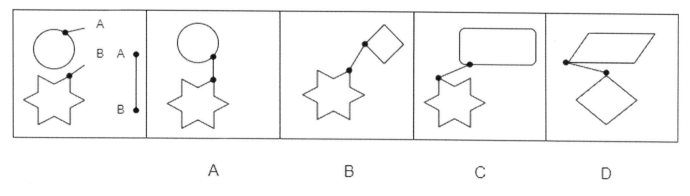

A   B   C   D

Figure 9.2: Example for a Combination Question

As represented by the figure, only option A entirely represents the shapes given in the original question. All the other options do not contain the same mathematical images. Hence, option A is the correct answer.

To prepare for these types of questions, it's beneficial to practice with puzzles, engage in activities that require spatial reasoning, and familiarize yourself with different perspectives and orientations of objects. Regular practice with mock questions similar to those in the Assembling Objects subtest can greatly enhance your spatial reasoning skills and improve your performance in this section of the ASVAB.

The Final Salute

As we fasten the last bolt on this chapter, it's clear that assembling objects is far more than a mere step-by-step process; it's an intricate dance of precision, safety, and spatial understanding. Whether it's the meticulous fitting of gears, the strategic sequencing of shelter construction, or the careful handling of tools, each aspect has underscored the importance of methodical and cautious workmanship.

What We've Achieved

The journey from interpreting blueprints to the hands-on assembly of complex systems is one of meticulous skill development. We have navigated through the essentials of tool selection, risk assessment, and safety — each element an integral cog in the machinery of mechanical comprehension. In military contexts, these skills translate to the ability to execute tasks with both finesse and fortitude, ensuring each mission is backed by the unwavering reliability of well-assembled equipment.

Why This Matters

For those preparing for the ASVAB, this chapter has not only equipped you with the knowledge to excel in the Assembling Objects section but has also laid the foundation for the practical application of these skills in a variety of military roles. The ability to visualize in three dimensions, select the appropriate tool for the task, and construct with both speed and safety is invaluable. It's a testament to the fact that the most robust structures are built on the smallest of details.

John's Final Words of Wisdom

In closing, remember that each component you assemble, each tool you wield, and each safety protocol you follow is a step toward a future where your skills contribute to a larger purpose. The discipline, patience, and precision you bring to each task will serve as your allies, not just in your quest to join the ranks of the military, but in every challenge you encounter beyond.

Carry these lessons forward, for they are the building blocks of a proficient servicemember, one who assembles with intent, operates with care, and executes with precision.

ASVAB TEST MINDSET

The importance of a focused and positive mindset when approaching the ASVAB cannot be overstated. This test is not merely a measure of your current knowledge but also a reflection of your potential for training and growth in the military. Cultivating the right mental approach is as crucial as mastering the test material.

Exam Overview
Understanding the Test Layout

The Armed Services Vocational Aptitude Battery (ASVAB) is a comprehensive examination designed to assess a candidate's aptitude and suitability for various roles in the U.S. Armed Forces. The exam covers a wide range of subjects, each designed to measure different abilities that are crucial in both military and civilian jobs. Understanding the layout and content of the ASVAB is key to effective preparation and success.

Content Areas

The ASVAB consists of the following subtests, each focusing on different skill sets:

- **General Science (GS):** Assesses knowledge of life science, earth and space science, and physical science.
- **Arithmetic Reasoning (AR):** Measures the ability to solve basic arithmetic word problems.
- **Word Knowledge (WK):** Tests the ability to understand the meaning of words through synonyms.
- **Paragraph Comprehension (PC):** Evaluates the ability to obtain information from written material.
- **Mathematics Knowledge (MK):** Measures knowledge of mathematical concepts and applications.
- **Electronics Information (EI):** Assesses knowledge of electrical circuits, batteries, and related terminology.
- **Auto Information (AI) and Shop Information (SI):** Tests knowledge of automotive maintenance and repair, and wood and metal shop practices.
- **Mechanical Comprehension (MC):** Measures understanding of basic mechanical and physical principles.
- **Assembling Objects (AO):** Assesses spatial ability through the visualization of how objects fit together.

Test Length and Timing

- **CAT-ASVAB:** The computerized version adapts to the test-taker's ability level. The number of questions and time allotted for each subtest vary, but the total testing time is approximately 1.5 to 2 hours.
- **P&P ASVAB:** This version has a fixed number of questions and set time limits for each subtest, typically taking about 3 hours to complete.

Scoring

- **AFQT Score:** The Armed Forces Qualifying Test score is derived from four subtests - AR, MK, WK, and PC. This score determines eligibility for enlistment.
- **Composite Scores:** These scores are calculated from different combinations of all subtests and are used to determine qualification for specific military occupations.

Test Day Preparation

- **Identification:** Bring valid identification to the testing center.
- **Materials:** For the P&P version, you may need pencils and an eraser. The CAT-ASVAB is completed entirely on the computer.
- **Personal Items:** Check the rules regarding personal items like watches, cell phones, and bags.

Mental Fortitude
Maintaining Calmness and Confidence

Approaching any test, especially one as significant as the ASVAB, requires more than just knowledge and preparation; it demands mental fortitude. The ability to maintain calmness and confidence under pressure is pivotal. This mental resilience not only influences your performance during the test but also reflects the psychological strength essential in military service.

Understanding Mental Fortitude

Mental fortitude is the capacity to remain composed and determined in challenging situations. It involves:

- **Stress Management:** The ability to handle pressure and anxiety without letting it overpower your focus.
- **Confidence:** Trusting in your preparation and abilities, even in the face of uncertainty.
- **Emotional Regulation:** Keeping your emotions in check, ensuring they don't negatively impact your decision-making or concentration.

Building Calmness

To cultivate a sense of calm:

- **Meditation and Breathing Exercises:** Regular practice can significantly reduce stress levels and improve concentration.
- **Visualization Techniques:** Envisioning success and positive outcomes can be a powerful tool for building confidence and reducing anxiety.
- **Stay in the Present:** Focus on the task at hand rather than worrying about future results or past mistakes.

Fostering Confidence

Building self-confidence involves:

- **Preparation:** Thoroughly preparing for the test is the foundation of confidence. Knowing you have done all you can to prepare should boost your self-assurance.

- **Positive Self-Talk:** Replace negative thoughts with positive affirmations. Remind yourself of your strengths and past successes.
- **Mock Tests:** Practice with simulated tests to familiarize yourself with the format and reduce fear of the unknown.

On the Day of the Test

- **Avoid Last-Minute Studying:** It can increase anxiety. Trust in your preparation and allow your mind to rest.
- **Healthy Routine:** Ensure you have a nutritious meal and stay hydrated. Avoid excessive caffeine, which can heighten anxiety.
- **Warm-Up Your Brain:** Engage in a light, non-stressful mental activity to get your brain into the right mode.

Post-Test Reflection

- **Self-Evaluation:** Reflect on your performance calmly. Focus on what you learned and how you can improve, rather than on any perceived failures.
- **Seek Feedback:** Constructive feedback can provide insights and areas for improvement in both knowledge and test-taking strategies.

Focus & Presence
Ensuring Full Engagement During the Test

The ability to fully engage and maintain focus throughout the ASVAB is a key component of test success. This means being present in the moment, concentrating on each question, and not allowing external or internal distractions to disrupt your train of thought. Developing this level of focus and presence is critical, not only for the test but also for future tasks and responsibilities in a military career.

Cultivating Focus

To achieve a high level of focus:

- **Eliminate Distractions:** Create a study environment free from interruptions. During the test, keep your attention on the screen or paper, avoiding wandering thoughts or glances.

- **Mindfulness Practices:** Regular mindfulness or meditation can train your brain to stay focused on the present moment, enhancing concentration and mental clarity.

Enhancing Presence

Being fully present during the test involves:

- **Active Engagement:** Read each question carefully and actively think about your response. Engaging with the material prevents mind wandering.
- **Breaking Down the Test:** Approach the test one question at a time, focusing solely on the question at hand rather than the entire test or its outcome.

Techniques to Maintain Focus

- **Regular Breaks During Study:** This helps prevent mental fatigue. During the test, take brief mental breaks between sections if possible
- **Practice Tests:** Simulate test conditions to get used to focusing for extended periods under exam-like conditions
- **Healthy Lifestyle Choices:** Adequate sleep, proper nutrition, and regular exercise can significantly improve concentration and cognitive function.

Time Management
Prioritizing Questions and Strategic Flagging

Time management is a crucial aspect of tackling the ASVAB, particularly given the varied complexity and length of different sections. Effective time management involves not just keeping track of the time but also making strategic decisions about how to allocate it across questions. This skill ensures that you can give your best to each section and maximize your overall score.

Prioritizing Questions

To effectively manage your time:

- **Quickly Assess Each Question:** Quickly read through each question and gauge its complexity.

- **Prioritize Easy Questions:** Answer simpler questions first. This approach can build confidence and ensures that you secure these points early in the test.
- **Mark and Return:** For more challenging questions, make a quick judgment call. If a question seems too time-consuming, mark it (if possible) and plan to return to it later.

Strategic Flagging

Many computer-based tests, including the CAT-ASVAB, allow you to flag questions:

- **Flag with Purpose:** Use the flagging feature to mark questions you are unsure about. This helps you easily find and review them later if time permits.
- **Balance Time:** Be mindful of the time you spend on flagged questions during your review. It's important to leave enough time to give each a fair second look

Managing Time Per Section

- **Understand Section Time Limits:** Familiarize yourself with the time allotted for each section of the ASVAB. This knowledge allows you to pace yourself appropriately.
- **Practice Timed Sessions:** While studying, simulate the test environment with timed practice sessions. This helps in understanding how much time to allocate per question.

Techniques for Quick Decision-Making

- **Eliminate Wrong Answers:** Even if you're unsure of the right answer, eliminating obviously incorrect options can increase your chances of guessing correctly.
- **Educated Guessing:** If you must guess, base your decision on any relevant knowledge or logical deductions you can make about the question

During the Test

- **Keep an Eye on the Clock:** Regularly check the time but avoid constantly watching the clock, as this can increase anxiety.

- **Adjust as Necessary:** If you find yourself spending too much time on a section, adjust your strategy and move more quickly through the remaining questions.

Post-Test

Review Your Approach: After the test, evaluate how well you managed your time. Consider what strategies worked well and where you might improve in future tests or tasks.

Handling Outcomes
Navigating Test Success and Setbacks

The outcome of the ASVAB can significantly impact your military career trajectory. It's crucial to approach both success and setbacks with a balanced perspective, using them as opportunities for growth and self-reflection. Let's explore how to navigate the aftermath of your test results, regardless of the outcome.

Celebrating Success

If you achieve a score that meets or exceeds your expectations:

- **Acknowledge Your Achievement:** Celebrate your success and recognize the hard work that led to this accomplishment.
- **Set Future Goals:** Use this achievement as a stepping stone for future goals. Consider the military career paths that your score opens up for you.
- **Share Your Experience:** Your journey can inspire and guide others. Share your study strategies and test experience with peers who are preparing for the ASVAB.

Dealing with Setbacks

If your score doesn't meet your expectations:

- **Stay Positive:** Understand that a setback is not a measure of your worth or potential. It's an opportunity to learn and grow.
- **Evaluate and Reflect:** Take time to assess what factors might have affected your performance. Was it preparation, test anxiety, or time management?

- **Develop a Plan:** Based on your reflection, create a plan for improvement. This might include additional study, focusing on weaker areas, or developing better test-taking strategies.

Seeking Feedback
Regardless of the outcome:

- **Seek Constructive Feedback:** Discuss your performance with a recruiter, teacher, or mentor. They can provide valuable insights and guidance.
- **Review the Test:** If possible, review the sections where you lost points to understand your mistakes.

Preparing for Retest or Next Steps

- **Retest Option:** If your score wasn't as high as needed for your desired military role, consider the option to retake the ASVAB.
- **Further Preparation:** Enhance your study plan focusing on areas of weakness. Utilize different study materials or methods if needed.

Embracing the Journey
Remember, the ASVAB is an important step, but it's just one part of your journey to a military career. Whether you're celebrating success or facing setbacks, each experience is a valuable lesson that prepares you for the challenges and triumphs of a life in service. Embrace each outcome as an opportunity for personal development and a steppingstone toward your future goals.

BONUS: 1-WEEK STUDY PLAN

Preparing for the ASVAB within a week calls for a dedicated and well-structured approach. This concise schedule aims to maximize your study time by strategically covering all key areas of the test, including mathematics, verbal skills, and technical knowledge. Each day focuses on different subjects, integrating practice tests and review sessions to reinforce learning and identify areas for improvement. This method ensures a thorough and efficient preparation for the diverse challenges of the exam.

DAY	Focus Areas	Morning (2 hrs)	Afternoon (2 hrs)	Evening (1 hr)
1	Initial Assessment and General Overview	Full-length ASVAB Simulation Test	Review test results: Identify Weak Areas	Introduction to Test Format and Question Types via Video Lessons
2	Mathematics & Verbal Skills (AR & MK / WK & PC)	Study AR and MK : Flashcards, Book, Video Lessons	Study WK and PC: Video Lessons, Flashcards	Practice Problems: AR, MK, WK, PC
3	Science & Technical I (GS & EI / AI & SI)	Study GS and EI: Book, Video Lessons	Study AI and SI: Practical Examples, Video Lessons	Practice Problems: GS, EI, AI, SI
4	Science & Technical II (MC & AO)	Study MC: Interactive Simulations, Book Chapters	Study AO: Spatial Exercises, Video Tutorials	Practice Problems: MC, AO
5	Comprehensive Review (All Areas)	Comprehensive Practice Test: All Sections	Review All Areas: Focus on Incorrect Responses	Light Review: Challenging Topics Across All Areas
6	Intensive Focus (Weak Areas)	Dedicated study: Weakest Areas (Flexible)	Continued Focused Study: Weakest Areas	Review and Practice: Selected Weak Areas
7	Final Review (All Areas)	Quick review: All sections, Key Summaries	Make Your Final Exam Simulation	Quick review: All sections, key summaries

Additional Tips:

Practice under real test conditions, maintain a healthy lifestyle with proper diet and sleep, stay positive, and include short breaks to avoid burnout. Adjust the plan according to your personal needs and strengths.

CONCLUSION

Embarking on Your Journey with Confidence

As we conclude this guide, it's important to reflect on the journey we've undertaken together. Preparing for the ASVAB is not just about acing a test; it's a step towards a future in the military, a commitment to serving your country, and a testament to your dedication and resilience. This guide has aimed to not only prepare you for the exam but also to equip you with skills and knowledge that will be valuable throughout your military career and beyond.

A Recap of the Journey

We've navigated through the various sections of the ASVAB, uncovering the intricacies of each topic and providing strategies for tackling them effectively. From understanding complex mathematical concepts to deciphering the mechanics of everyday objects, we've covered a vast landscape of knowledge. We've also delved into strategies for maintaining focus, managing time, and handling the outcomes of the test, all crucial skills for any aspiring service member.

The Bigger Picture

Remember, the ASVAB is not just an assessment of your current abilities; it's a tool to help place you where your skills and talents can be best utilized in the military. It's about finding your fit in a larger mission, contributing your unique abilities towards something greater than yourself.

Moving Forward

As you close this guide and move forward:

- *Continue Learning:* Your journey of learning and self-improvement doesn't end here. Keep expanding your knowledge and skills.
- *Stay Determined:* The path to achieving your goals may have challenges, but your perseverance will see you through.
- *Embrace Opportunities:* The military offers a world of opportunities for growth, leadership, and personal development. Embrace these chances wholeheartedly.

Final Words

You stand on the threshold of an incredible journey, one that will challenge you, shape you, and offer opportunities to make a meaningful impact. As you take this step forward, do so with confidence, knowing that you have prepared to the best of your ability. Your dedication, skills, and the knowledge you've gained from this guide are the tools that will help you succeed in the ASVAB and in your future endeavors in the military.

Best of luck and may this be just the beginning of a rewarding and fulfilling journey.

Ryan MacArmen

Support

For any eventuality do not hesitate to contact my support at this email:
info@speedprepacademy.com

My team will be happy to assist you!

Made in the USA
Columbia, SC
05 February 2025

ef32480b-be64-4256-8e01-989ed7c06901R01